Preface

The study of algorithms is fundamental to the field of computer science and engineering, and it forms the backbone of software development, data processing, and problem-solving. The course MCS-211: Design and Analysis of Algorithms, offered by the Indira Gandhi National Open University (IGNOU), is pivotal for students pursuing a degree in computer science. The rigorous curriculum of this course requires students to not only understand the theoretical aspects of algorithms but also to apply this knowledge in solving complex computational problems. To assist students in their journey of mastering this subject, this book presents a comprehensive collection of previous years' unsolved papers of the MCS-211 course.The rationale behind compiling these unsolved papers is to provide students with a valuable resource that will enhance their understanding of the subject and prepare them effectively for examinations. These papers serve as an essential tool for self-assessment, allowing students to gauge their knowledge, identify areas that require further study, and practice solving problems within the time constraints typically imposed by examinations. Moreover, working through these papers helps students develop the analytical thinking and problem-solving skills necessary to excel in the field of algorithms.

This book is meticulously organized to cater to the needs of students at various levels of understanding. Each paper included in this compilation is carefully selected from different years to represent a broad spectrum of topics covered in the MCS-211 syllabus. The problems range from basic algorithmic challenges to more complex scenarios that test a student's ability to design efficient and effective algorithms. By attempting these unsolved papers, students will not only reinforce their theoretical knowledge but also gain hands-on experience in tackling real-world algorithmic problems.In addition to serving as an academic resource, this book is also intended to instill confidence in students as they prepare for their examinations. The exposure to a variety of problems will familiarize students with the types of questions that are likely to appear in exams, enabling them to approach their studies with a strategic mindset. This book encourages a deeper exploration of the subject, prompting students to engage with the material beyond the standard textbook content and to think critically about the design and analysis of algorithms.

We would like to express our gratitude to the students and educators who have contributed to the development of this book. Their insights and feedback have been invaluable in ensuring that this compilation meets the highest standards of academic excellence. As you embark on your journey through the world of algorithms, we hope that this book will be a reliable companion in your studies, helping you to unlock the full potential of your capabilities in the field of computer science.

Table of Contents

MCS – 211

Master Of Computer Applications (MCA-New)
Chapter 1: Term-End Examination, December, 2021
MCS-211: Design and Analysis of Algorithms

Time: 3 Hours
Maximum Marks: 100
(Weightage: 70%)

Note: (i) Question No. 1 is compulsory.
(ii) Attempt any three Questions from the rest.

1. (a) Write a mathematical definition of O (big oh). Assume that the function f(n) = 2n2 + 3n + 1. Show that f(n) = O(n2). 5

(b) Define a recurrence relation of QuickSort algorithm and solve it using a recurrence tree. 10

(c) What are the key features of combinatorial problems? Describe and formulate three combinatorial problems. 10

(d) Describe a task scheduling problem as an optimization problem. Apply the scheduling algorithm with deadlines to maximize the total profit to the following problem: 10

Jobs	Deadlines	Profits
1	2	60
2	3	50
3	4	70
4	5	80
5	4	75
6	3	55
7	2	40

(e) List all the different orders in which we can multiply five matrices M1, M2, M3, M4, M5. 10

2. (a) Explain the naïve string matching algorithm and derive its worst case complexity. What is its drawback? What will be the maximum valid shifts of a pattern in the text in the following example? 10

Text: a b c x y z d e f g h

Pattern: f g h

(b) What is the similarity between Dijkstra's single source shortest path and Prim's minimum cost spanning tree algorithms? Apply Dijkstra's algorithm to find the shortest path from v1 to all other vertices of the following graph: 10

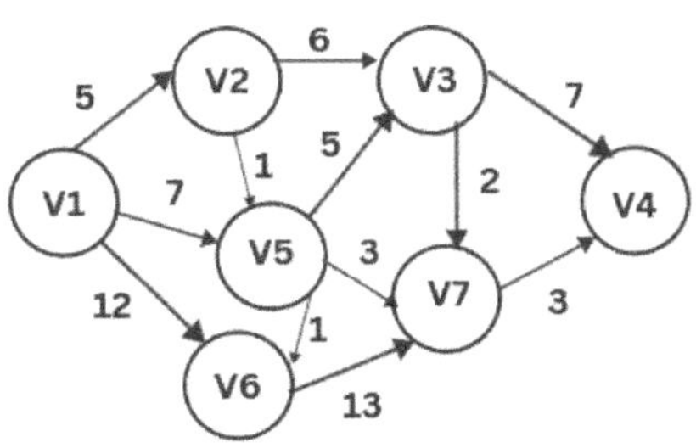

3. (a) Apply Horner's method for evaluating a polynomial expression $p(x) = 6x6 + 5x5 + 4x4 - 3x3 + 8x - 7$ at $x = 3$. Calculate: 10

(i) How many times will the loop execute?

(ii) What will be the total number of multiplication and addition operations?

(b) Define a fractional knapsack problem as an optimization problem. Write a greedy method to find an optimal solution to the problem. Show the complexity of the algorithm. 10

4. (a) Apply the DFS algorithm to the following graph with the starting vertex v1 . List the order in which vertices will be visited.

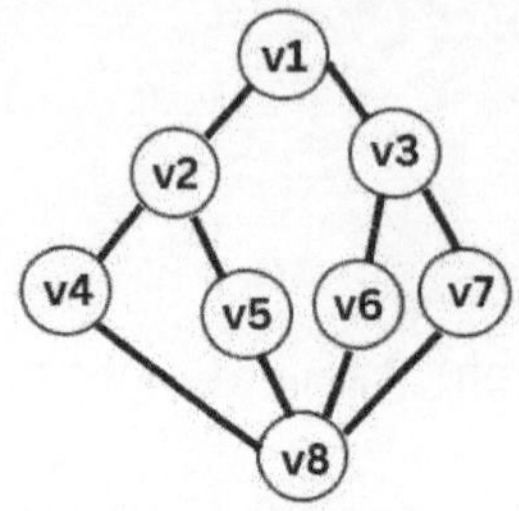

Show the complexity analysis if a graph is represented through

(i) Adjacency list, and

(ii) Adjacency matrix. 10

(b) Explain P, NP and NP-complete class of problems with appropriate examples of each class. 10

5. (a) Apply Floyd Warshall's algorithm and show the matrix D2 of the following graph: 10

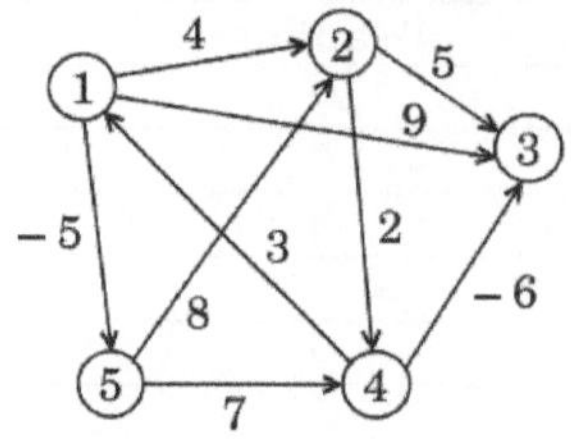

(b) Explain the use of master method. Write and interpret all the three cases of the master method to solve recurrence relation problem.

MCS – 211

Master Of Computer Applications (MCA-New)
Chapter 2: Term-End Examination, June, 2022
MCS-211: Design and Analysis of Algorithms

Time: 3 Hours
Maximum Marks: 100
(Weightage: 70%)

Note: (i) Question No. 1 is compulsory.
(ii) Attempt any three Questions from the rest.

1.(a)Calculate the time complexity of thefollowing program fragments using Big Ohnotation: 5

(i)
```
For(i=0;i<n;i++)
a[i]=0;
for(i=0;i<n;i++)
for(j=0,j<n;j++);A[i]=A[i]+A[j]
```

(ii)
```
For(i=1;i≤n;i=i*2).
{
x =x +i;
}
```

(b)Explain the working principle of Floyd-Warshall's algorithm. 5

(c)Define topological ordering of a graph.Write the algorithm to find topologicalordering of the following graph.Calculatethe complexity of the algorithm: 10

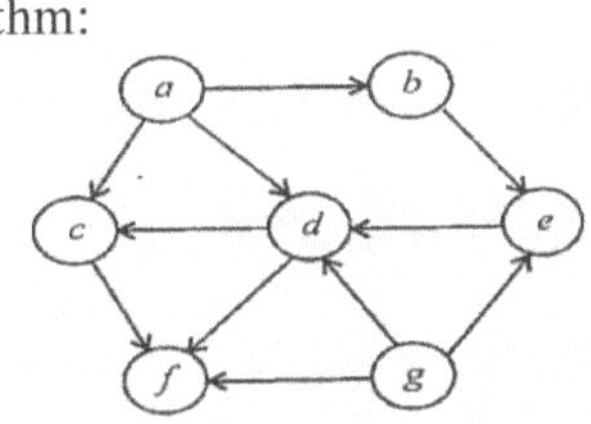

(d)Define the substitution method to solve arecurrence relation.Solve the following recurrence relationusing substitution method: 10

$$T(n)=2T(n12)+n$$

(e)Write Kruskal's algorithm to findminimum cost spanning tree of thefollowing graph: 10

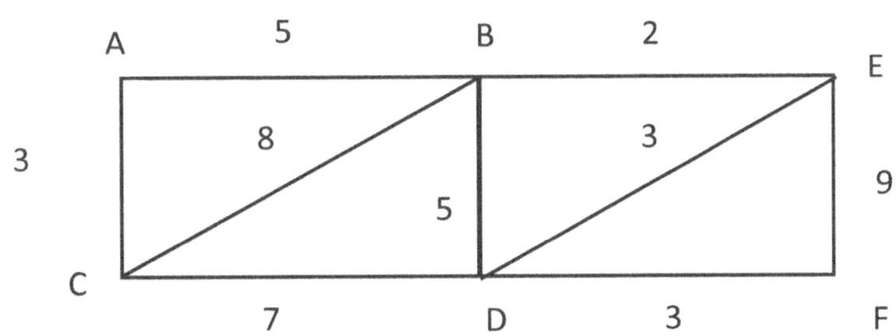

Show complexity analysis of the algorithmand all the intermediate steps.

2.(a)Describe the most commonly used datastructure for implementing Dijkstra singlesource shortest path algorithm. 5

(b)Prove that "Subpaths of the shortest pathin a single source shortest path algorithmare also the shortest paths." 5

(c)Apply Bubble sort algorithm for thefollowing list of numbers: 10

12	65	45	15	25	30	20	18	7

Calculate its best case and worst case timecomplexities.

3.(a)Write and explain the procedure to find asolution to maximum bipartite matchingproblem with the help of an example. 7

(b)List one algorithm each for the followingtime complexities: 3
(i) O(m logn)
(ii) O(logn)
(iii) $O(n^2)$

(c)Find the optimal solution to the followinginstance of a fractional Knapsack problem.Show step-by-step running of thealgorithm: 10
Number of objects =5
Capacity of a knapsack W=15
Pi=Profit of an object i
wi=Weight of an object i
$(P_1,P_2,P_3,P_4,P_5) = (15,30,40,35,55)$
$(w_1,w_2,w_3,w_4,w_5) = (5,9,3,7,2)$

4.(a)Explain the concept of rolling hashfunction applied in Rabin-Karp algorithmfor string matching problem with the helpof an example. 10

(b)Differentiate between greedy approach anddynamic approach to solve an optimizationproblem. 4

(c)Formulate the following problemsasoptimization and decision problems: 6
(i)Traveling salesperson problem
(i)Graph coloring problem

5.(a)Explain the concept of non-deterministicalgorithm with the help of an example.Listtheproblems which belong to non-deterministic class of complexity. 8

(b)Whether the following is in correctorder? 2

1, log n, n nlog n, n^2, 2^n n!

(c)Construct an optimal Huffman tree andHuffman code for each character for thefollowing set of frequencies:

A:20, B:25, C:10, D:8, E:7, F:12, G:10.

Show all the intermediate steps. 10

MCS – 211

Master Of Computer Applications (MCA-New)
Chapter 3: Term-End Examination, December, 2022
MCS-211: Design and Analysis of Algorithms

Time: 3 Hours
Maximum Marks: 100
(Weightage: 70%)

Note: (i) Question No. 1 is compulsory.
(ii) Attempt any three Questions from the rest.

1. (a) Write a mathematical definition of big omega (Ω). For the functions defined by $f(n) = 3n3 + 2n2 + 1$ and $g(n) = 2n2 + 3$, verify that $f(n) = \Omega(g(n))$. 6

(b) Explain the principle of optimality in dynamic programming, with the help of an example. 6

(c) Apply a master method to give the tight asymptotic bounds of the following recurrences: 8
(i) $T(n) = 4T(n/2) + n2$
(ii) $T(n) = 9T(n/3) + n$

(d) Run the Prim's algorithm on the following graph. Assume that the root vertex is **a**.

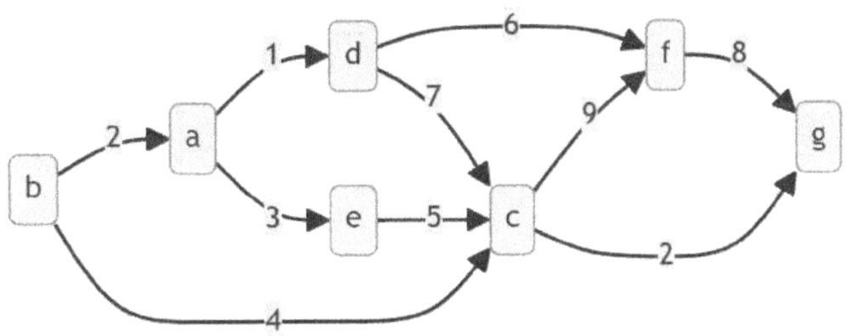

Derive the complexity of the algorithm. 10

(e) Apply Huffman's algorithm to construct a Huffman's tree and optimal binary prefix code for the letters and its frequencies as given in the following table: 10

Letter	Frequency
A	15
B	6
C	7
D	5
E	12
I	13
Z	2

2. (a) Explain Cook-Levin's theorem on CNF-Safisfiability problem, with the help of an example. 10

(b) (i) Apply Dijkstra's single source shortest path algorithm to the following graph with **a** as starting vertex. Show all the intermediate steps.

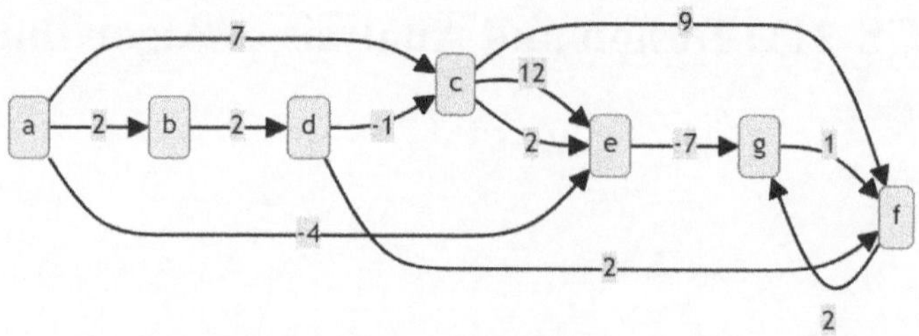

(ii) What is the significant feature of Bellman-Ford's algorithm which is not supported in Dijkstra's algorithm? 3

3. (a) Write and explain pseudocode for Ford-Fulkerson's algorithm for maximum bipartite matching. 10

(b) Apply the partition procedure of Quicksort algorithm to the following array: [35, 10, 40, 5, 60, 25, 45, 15] Show all the intermediate steps. 10

4. (a) Apply DFS to the complete graph on four vertices. List the vertices in the order they would be visited. 7

(b) How many comparisons are needed for a binary search in a set of 512 elements? 3

(c) Apply Floyd-Warshall's algorithm to the following graph and show D2 . 10

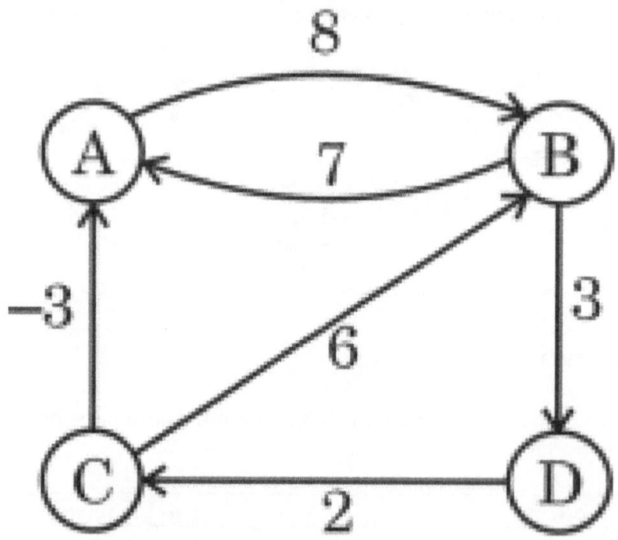

5. (a) Describe the task scheduling algorithm as an optimization problem and calculate its complexity. Consider the following jobs and its service times and apply the task scheduling algorithm to minimize the total amount of time spent in the system. 10

Letter	Frequency
1	10
2	15
3	8

4	12
5	6

(b) Describe the basic principle of KMP algorithm for string matching. What is its advantage compared to Naive and Rabin-Karp's algorithm for string matching? Calculate the time complexity of KMP algorithm. 10

MCS – 211

Master Of Computer Applications (MCA-New)
Chapter 4: Term-End Examination, June, 2023
MCS-211: Design and Analysis of Algorithms

Time: 3 Hours
Maximum Marks: 100
(Weightage: 70%)

Note: (i) Question No. 1 is compulsory.
(ii) Attempt any three Questions from the rest.

1. (a) What is an algorithm? What are its desirable characteristics? 5

(b) What are asymptotic notations? Explain any two asymptotic notations with suitable example for each. 5

(c) Solve the following recurrence relation using substitution method: 5

$$T(n) = 2T(n/2) + n$$

(d) Write and explain binary search algorithm with an suitable example. 5

(e) Explain Depth First Search (DFS) algorithm with an suitable example. 5

(f) What is Dynamic Programming approach of problem solving? Write the steps involved in dynamic programming. 6

(g) What are Optimization and Decision problems? Give an example of each. 5

(h) Design a state space tree for the given subset sum problem. S = {4, 6, 7, 8}, W = 8. 4

3. (a) Explain all the three cases of Master's Theorem. Apply Master's theorem to solve the given recurrence relation: $T(n) = 9T(n/3)$ 8

(b) Evaluate:

$$p(x)=3x^4+2x^3-5x+7 \text{at } x=2$$

Using Horner's rule. Show stepwise iterations.

(c) Prove that for all non-negative integers 'n': 6
□ 2^0 +2^1 +2^2 + ...2^n = 2^(n+1) - 1.

3. (a) What is Huffman coding? Write the steps for building the Huffman tree with an example. 6

(b) Explain Quick sort algorithm using divide and conquer approach. 6

(c) What are strongly connected components? Explain how adjacency matrix and adjacency list are created for a connected graph with the help of a suitable diagram. 2+3+3

4. (a) Show the step by step execution of Kruskal's algorithm for the following graph: 6

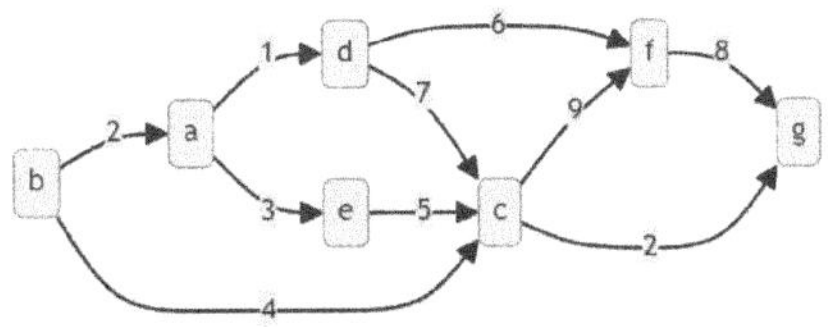

(b) What is Matrix chain multiplication problem? Find an optimal parenthesization of a martix-chain product whose sequence of dimensions are as follows: 2+6

Matrix	Matrix
A1	30 X 35
A2	35 X 15
A3	15 X 5

(c) Explain Rabin Karp Algorithm for string matching with suitable example. 6

5. Write short notes on any four of the following:
4×5=20

(i) Deterministic vs. Non-deterministic algorithms
(ii) CLIQUE and vertex cover problem
(iii) Backtracking problem with example
(iv) Bellman-Ford algorithm
(v) Fractional Knapsack problem

MCS – 211

Master Of Computer Applications (MCA-New)
Chapter 5: Term-End Examination, December, 2023
MCS-211: Design and Analysis of Algorithms

Time: 3 Hours
Maximum Marks: 100
(Weightage: 70%)

Note: (i) Question No. 1 is compulsory.
(ii) Attempt any three Questions from the rest.

1. (a) What is Euclid's algorithm to find GCD of two given integers? Write the steps involved in finding GCD of (a, b) using Euclid's algorithm. 5

(b) What are Big 'O' and Big 'Θ' notations? Explain with the help of representative diagram. 5

(c) Write and explain linear search algorithm. Mention best case, worst case and average case scenarios of linear search. 5

(d) Explain Breadth First Search (BFS) algorithm with a suitable example. 5

(e) What is Task Scheduling algorithm? Write pseudo code for task scheduling algorithm. 5

(f) Solve the given recurrence relation using recursion tree method: 5

$$\square(n) = 2T(n/2) + n$$

□ □

(g) What are P, NP and NP-complete problems? Give example of each. 5

(h) What is a Minimum Cost Spanning Tree (MCST)? Write Generic MCST algorithm. 5

2. (a) What are the building blocks of an algorithm? Explain how to judge an algorithm, whether it is efficient or not? 6

(b) Using mathematical induction, prove that the sum of first 'n' positive integers is [n(n+1)/2] i.e $1 + 2 + 3 \ldots\ldots\ldots + n = n(n+1)/2$ 6

(c) What is polynomial evaluation? What are its methods of evaluation? Evaluate $P(x)=3x^2+5x+6$using Horner's rule at x=3. 2+2+4

3. (a) What is Greedy approach for problem solving? How does a Greedy algorithm work? Write the activities performed in Greedy method. 6

(b) Explain merge sort algorithm using divide and conquer approach. Also mention its best case and worst case time complexities. 6+2

(c) Explain any three of the following terms with the help of a suitable diagram: 3×2=6
(i) Subgraph
(ii) Connected graph
(iii) Adjacency matrix
(iv) Directed acyclic graph

4. (a) Show the step by step execution of Dijkstra's single source shortest path algorithm on the given directed graph from source vertex '**a**': 6

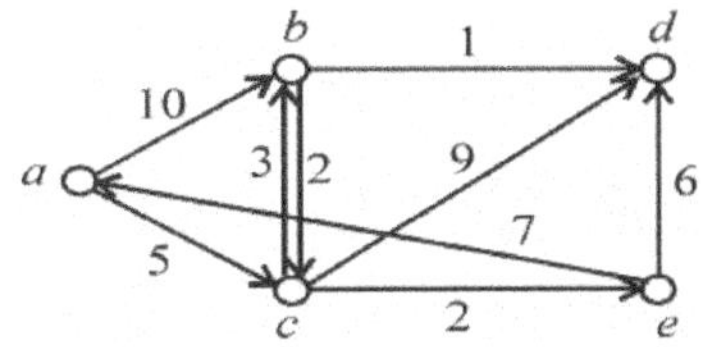

(b) What is string matching problem? Explain Knuth Morris Pratt algorithm of string matching with a suitable example. Explain the process of building LPS array for a pattern 'P'. 2+4+2

(c) What is all pair shortest path problem? Write and explain Floyd Warshall algorithm for shortest paths with the help of a diagram. 6

5. Write short notes on any four of the following: 4×5=20

(i) Tractable vs. Intractable problems
(ii) CNF Satisfiability problem
(iii) Optimization and decision problems
(iv) Prim's algorithm
(v) Approximation algorithms
(vi) Master's theorem

Chapter 6: Most Asked Questions Part-A

1. What is an algorithm and why is it important in computer science?
Answer: An algorithm is a finite, step-by-step set of well-defined instructions used to perform a specific task or solve a particular problem. It is fundamental in computer science because it provides a clear procedure for computation, enabling programs to function efficiently. Algorithms are used in a wide range of applications such as searching, sorting, optimization, machine learning, and network routing. Their effectiveness is measured in terms of time and space complexity. Understanding algorithms allows developers to write better code, optimize performance, and tackle complex problems systematically. They are crucial for developing scalable and efficient software systems.

2. What are the main characteristics of a good algorithm?
Answer: A good algorithm possesses several essential characteristics: it must be correct, meaning it provides accurate results for all valid inputs; it must be finite, meaning it terminates after a limited number of steps; and it must be unambiguous, with clear and understandable instructions. Additionally, a good algorithm is efficient, optimizing time and space usage. It should also be general enough to solve a class of related problems rather than a specific instance. Lastly, a good algorithm should be easy to understand, implement, and maintain. These characteristics ensure the algorithm is practical and reliable for real-world applications.

3. What is time complexity and how is it measured?
Answer: Time complexity is a computational metric that describes the amount of time an algorithm takes to run as a function of the size of its input. It is typically measured using Big O notation, which expresses the upper bound of the running time in terms of input size nnn. Common time complexities include O(1), O(log n), O(n), O(n log n), O(n^2), and so on. Time complexity helps compare different algorithms and choose the most efficient one for a given problem. It does not reflect actual execution time but gives an estimation based on input growth.

4. What is space complexity in algorithm analysis?
Answer: Space complexity refers to the total amount of memory an algorithm requires to complete its execution, relative to the size of the input data. This includes the memory needed for input values, auxiliary variables, temporary storage, and function calls (especially in recursive algorithms). Space complexity is also measured using Big O notation, such as O(1) for constant space or O(n) for linear space. Understanding space complexity is vital for systems with limited memory or where resource optimization is critical. Balancing time and space complexity is a key challenge in algorithm design and optimization.

5. What is the difference between worst-case, best-case, and average-case time complexity?
Answer: Worst-case time complexity represents the maximum time an algorithm could take to complete, given the most unfavorable input. Best-case refers to the minimum time required when the input is in the most favorable condition. Average-case time complexity provides an expected run time for random inputs, based on probabilistic analysis. While worst-case analysis guarantees performance limits, average-case often reflects typical behavior. Best-case, though informative, is rarely used for performance guarantees. Understanding all three helps in choosing appropriate algorithms under different practical constraints and gives a holistic view of algorithm performance.

6. Explain Big O, Big Theta, and Big Omega notations.
Answer: Big O notation describes the upper bound of an algorithm's time or space complexity, indicating the worst-case scenario. Big Omega (Ω) notation provides the lower bound, representing the best-case performance. Big Theta (Θ) notation gives a tight bound, meaning it describes both the upper and lower limits for the algorithm's growth rate. For example, if an algorithm has Θ(n log n) time complexity, it performs no worse than O(n log n) and no better than Ω(n log n). These notations are essential in theoretical computer science for analyzing and comparing algorithm efficiency rigorously.

7. What is recursion and how does it work in algorithms?
Answer: Recursion is a programming technique where a function calls itself directly or indirectly to solve a problem. Each recursive call solves a smaller instance of the original problem until it reaches a base case, which terminates the recursion. Recursion simplifies problems like tree traversal, factorial computation, and Fibonacci series generation. It relies heavily on the system's call stack, which may lead to high memory usage or stack overflow if not properly

managed. Understanding recursion is crucial for solving divide-and-conquer problems and requires careful implementation of base conditions and recursive logic to ensure correctness.

8. What is the difference between iterative and recursive algorithms?
Answer: Iterative algorithms use loops (such as for, while) to repeat a set of instructions until a condition is met, whereas recursive algorithms solve a problem by calling themselves with smaller sub-problems. Recursive algorithms are often more elegant and easier to understand, especially for problems involving hierarchical or nested structures like trees. However, they may consume more memory due to call stack usage. Iterative solutions are generally more memory-efficient and sometimes faster. Both approaches have their place in algorithm design, and the choice depends on factors like clarity, resource constraints, and problem nature.

9. What is the divide and conquer approach in algorithm design?
Answer: Divide and conquer is an algorithm design paradigm that breaks a problem into smaller sub-problems, solves each recursively, and then combines the results to solve the original problem. It is effective for problems that can be naturally partitioned, such as merge sort, quicksort, and binary search. This approach improves efficiency by reducing the problem size at each step, often leading to logarithmic or linearithmic time complexities. Divide and conquer also facilitates parallel processing, making it suitable for large-scale computational problems. Its success depends on the efficiency of the divide, solve, and combine phases.

10. What are asymptotic notations and why are they important in algorithm analysis?
Answer: Asymptotic notations describe the behavior of an algorithm's running time or space requirements as the input size approaches infinity. The three main types are Big O (upper bound), Big Omega (lower bound), and Big Theta (tight bound). These notations allow computer scientists to abstract away machine-dependent constants and focus on how algorithms scale. They help in comparing algorithms and choosing the most efficient one for large inputs. Asymptotic notations are foundational in theoretical computer science, enabling the analysis and classification of algorithms based on their growth rates under limiting conditions.

11. What is the difference between a greedy algorithm and dynamic programming?
Answer: A greedy algorithm builds a solution step by step by choosing the locally optimal option at each step, aiming for a global optimum. It does not revisit previous decisions. Dynamic programming, on the other hand, solves problems by breaking them into overlapping subproblems and storing solutions to these subproblems to avoid recomputation. Greedy algorithms are generally faster and simpler but may not always yield the best solution for all problems. Dynamic programming guarantees optimal solutions for problems with optimal substructure and overlapping subproblems, though it may consume more memory and processing time.

12. What are the key features of divide and conquer algorithms?
Answer: Divide and conquer algorithms work by recursively breaking a problem into smaller subproblems, solving each independently, and combining their results to solve the original problem. The three key phases are: divide, conquer, and combine. This strategy is efficient for problems like merge sort, quicksort, and binary search. It reduces the time complexity and improves performance through parallelism and recursion. The effectiveness depends on how well the problem can be divided and the cost of combining sub-results. It is widely used for problems that naturally fit recursive decomposition.

13. How does the quicksort algorithm work?
Answer: Quicksort is a divide and conquer algorithm that sorts an array by selecting a 'pivot' element and partitioning the other elements into two sub-arrays—those less than the pivot and those greater. These sub-arrays are then recursively sorted. The key operation in quicksort is partitioning, which rearranges elements so that all smaller elements precede the pivot and larger ones follow. Quicksort has an average time complexity of O(n log n), making it efficient for large datasets. However, its worst-case time complexity is $O(n^2)$, which occurs when the pivot selection is poor.

14. What is the time complexity of merge sort and how does it compare to quicksort?
Answer: Merge sort has a consistent time complexity of O(n log n) in all cases—best, average, and worst. It divides the array into halves, recursively sorts each half, and then merges them back in sorted order. Unlike quicksort, merge sort's performance does not degrade with poor pivot selection. However, merge sort requires additional memory for

merging, which can be a disadvantage. In contrast, quicksort typically performs faster in practice due to better cache utilization and in-place sorting but may degrade to $O(n^2)$ without a good pivot strategy.

15. What is backtracking and where is it used?
Answer: Backtracking is an algorithmic paradigm used for solving problems incrementally by trying partial solutions and then abandoning them if they do not lead to a feasible solution. It is especially useful in constraint satisfaction problems and combinatorial search problems such as the N-Queens problem, Sudoku, and maze solving. The algorithm recursively explores options, backtracks upon reaching a dead-end, and tries alternative paths. Although it can be inefficient in the worst-case, pruning techniques like forward checking can improve performance. It ensures completeness and is often used when brute-force methods are impractical.

16. What are asymptotic notations in algorithm analysis?
Answer: Asymptotic notations are mathematical tools used to describe the running time or space requirement of an algorithm in terms of input size. The three primary notations are: Big O (O), which represents the upper bound or worst-case complexity; Omega (Ω), which denotes the lower bound or best-case complexity; and Theta (Θ), which indicates the tight bound or average-case complexity. These notations help compare the efficiency of algorithms by abstracting hardware and implementation details. They are crucial in theoretical computer science for analyzing scalability and performance.

17. What is a recurrence relation in algorithm design?
Answer: A recurrence relation is an equation or inequality that defines a function recursively in terms of its values on smaller inputs. In algorithm analysis, recurrence relations are used to describe the time complexity of recursive algorithms. For example, the recurrence for merge sort is $T(n) = 2T(n/2) + O(n)$. Solving these relations, often using methods like the substitution method, recursion tree, or master theorem, provides insights into algorithm efficiency. Understanding and solving recurrence relations is vital for analyzing the performance of divide and conquer algorithms.

18. What is memoization in dynamic programming?
Answer: Memoization is a technique used in dynamic programming to store the results of expensive function calls and reuse them when the same inputs occur again. It avoids redundant computations by caching the results of subproblems. This is especially useful in recursive algorithms that solve overlapping subproblems. Memoization can be implemented using arrays, hash maps, or dictionaries, depending on the language and problem. It transforms exponential time algorithms into polynomial time by preventing recomputation. This approach contrasts with tabulation, which solves problems iteratively from the bottom up.

19. What are graph traversal algorithms and their applications?
Answer: Graph traversal algorithms explore nodes and edges of a graph. The two main types are Depth-First Search (DFS) and Breadth-First Search (BFS). DFS explores as far as possible along a branch before backtracking, using a stack (often implemented recursively). BFS explores neighbors level by level using a queue. These algorithms are fundamental for tasks like pathfinding, cycle detection, topological sorting, and connectivity checking. They are widely used in areas such as social networks, web crawling, AI, and network routing. Each algorithm has its use depending on the graph structure and requirements.

20. What is the role of the Master Theorem in algorithm analysis?
Answer: The Master Theorem provides a straightforward way to determine the time complexity of divide and conquer algorithms with recurrence relations of the form $T(n) = aT(n/b) + f(n)$, where $a \geq 1$ and $b > 1$. It categorizes problems into three cases based on the relationship between f(n) and n^log_b(a), allowing quick derivation of asymptotic bounds. This theorem simplifies analysis without solving recurrences from scratch. It is particularly useful in analyzing algorithms like merge sort and binary search. Understanding its application is essential for efficient algorithm design.

21. How does the binary search algorithm work and what is its time complexity?
Answer: Binary search is an efficient algorithm used to find an element in a sorted array. It works by repeatedly dividing the search interval in half. Starting with the entire array, the algorithm compares the target value with the middle element. If they are equal, the search is complete. If the target is less, the search continues in the left sub-array;

if greater, in the right sub-array. This process continues until the target is found or the interval becomes empty. The time complexity of binary search is O(log n), making it highly efficient for large datasets.

22. What is the difference between BFS and DFS in graph traversal?

Answer: BFS (Breadth-First Search) and DFS (Depth-First Search) are two fundamental graph traversal techniques. BFS uses a queue to explore nodes level by level, ensuring the shortest path in unweighted graphs. DFS uses a stack or recursion to explore as far down a branch as possible before backtracking. BFS is useful for shortest path and level-order traversal, while DFS is preferred for topological sorting and detecting cycles in directed graphs. BFS generally uses more memory, while DFS can risk stack overflow on deep graphs. The choice depends on the problem's nature and graph structure.

23. What is the greedy method in algorithm design?

Answer: The greedy method is a problem-solving approach that builds a solution piece by piece, choosing the most optimal option at each step. It assumes that local optimization will lead to global optimization. Greedy algorithms are simple and efficient for problems like the fractional knapsack, activity selection, and Huffman coding. However, they do not always produce the optimal solution for all problems, unlike dynamic programming. The greedy method is effective when the problem exhibits the greedy-choice property and optimal substructure. It's valued for its speed and simplicity in appropriate scenarios.

24. What is a topological sort in graph algorithms?

Answer: Topological sort is an ordering of vertices in a Directed Acyclic Graph (DAG) such that for every directed edge u → v, vertex u appears before v in the ordering. It is used in scenarios involving dependency resolution, such as task scheduling, build systems, and course prerequisites. Algorithms like Kahn's algorithm (BFS-based) and DFS-based approaches can be used to perform topological sorting. It's only possible on DAGs, as the presence of cycles makes topological ordering impossible. The time complexity is O(V + E), where V is vertices and E is edges.

25. What is the difference between Prim's and Kruskal's algorithms?

Answer: Prim's and Kruskal's algorithms are both used to find the Minimum Spanning Tree (MST) of a connected, weighted graph. Prim's algorithm starts with a single node and grows the MST by adding the smallest edge connecting the tree to a new vertex. It uses a priority queue and is efficient for dense graphs. Kruskal's algorithm sorts all edges by weight and adds them to the MST if they don't form a cycle, typically using a union-find structure. Kruskal's is better suited for sparse graphs. Both have a time complexity of O(E log V).

26. What is the dynamic programming approach and when is it preferred?

Answer: Dynamic programming is a method for solving complex problems by breaking them down into simpler overlapping subproblems. It stores the results of subproblems to avoid redundant computation, making it efficient for problems with optimal substructure and overlapping subproblems. It is preferred when brute-force or recursive methods are inefficient due to recomputation. Problems like Fibonacci sequence, knapsack problem, and matrix chain multiplication are classic examples. There are two main approaches: top-down with memoization and bottom-up with tabulation. It typically improves exponential time complexity to polynomial.

27. What is a hash table and what are its applications in algorithms?

Answer: A hash table is a data structure that stores key-value pairs and provides fast access to data using a hash function. It maps keys to indices in an array, allowing constant-time complexity O(1) for insertions, deletions, and lookups on average. In algorithms, hash tables are used for quick access to data, frequency counting, caching, and implementing associative arrays. They are crucial in problems like detecting duplicates, anagrams, or storing memoized values in dynamic programming. However, performance depends on a good hash function and collision handling strategies like chaining or open addressing.

28. How does the Floyd-Warshall algorithm work?

Answer: The Floyd-Warshall algorithm is used to find the shortest paths between all pairs of vertices in a weighted graph. It works by initializing the distance between each pair of vertices with the weight of the direct edge, or infinity if none exists. Then it iteratively updates these distances by considering each vertex as an intermediate point. If a shorter path is found through an intermediate vertex, the distance is updated. The algorithm has a time complexity of $O(V^3)$ and works well for dense graphs. It also detects negative cycles when applied with proper checks.

29. What is the purpose of Dijkstra's algorithm?
Answer: Dijkstra's algorithm finds the shortest path from a source vertex to all other vertices in a graph with non-negative edge weights. It uses a priority queue to select the next closest vertex and updates the distances to neighboring vertices if a shorter path is found. The algorithm guarantees the shortest path and is efficient with a time complexity of $O((V + E) \log V)$ when using a min-heap. It is widely used in network routing, GPS navigation systems, and graph-based optimization problems where all edge weights are non-negative.

30. What are NP-complete problems in algorithm theory?
Answer: NP-complete problems are a class of decision problems for which no known polynomial-time algorithm exists but whose solutions can be verified in polynomial time. These problems are in both NP (nondeterministic polynomial time) and are as hard as any problem in NP. If any NP-complete problem can be solved in polynomial time, all NP problems can be. Examples include the traveling salesman problem, knapsack problem, and Boolean satisfiability (SAT). These problems are central to computational theory and are used to understand the limits of algorithmic solvability.

31. What is the Bellman-Ford algorithm and how does it differ from Dijkstra's algorithm?
Answer: The Bellman-Ford algorithm finds the shortest paths from a single source vertex to all other vertices in a weighted graph. Unlike Dijkstra's algorithm, it can handle graphs with negative edge weights. It works by repeatedly relaxing all edges, updating the shortest path estimates. It does this $|V| - 1$ times, where $|V|$ is the number of vertices. If further relaxation is possible after these iterations, it indicates a negative weight cycle. The time complexity is $O(VE)$. Bellman-Ford is preferred over Dijkstra when negative weights are present, despite being slower.

32. What is the difference between Divide and Conquer and Dynamic Programming?
Answer: Divide and Conquer divides a problem into independent subproblems, solves each recursively, and combines their solutions. Classic examples include Merge Sort and Quick Sort. Dynamic Programming also divides a problem into subproblems, but these subproblems overlap. It solves each once and stores their solutions, avoiding redundant work. While both use recursion, Dynamic Programming uses memoization or tabulation to enhance efficiency. Divide and Conquer is best for problems with non-overlapping subproblems, while DP is ideal for problems with optimal substructure and overlapping subproblems, like the Fibonacci series or matrix chain multiplication.

33. What is backtracking and where is it used in algorithm design?
Answer: Backtracking is a recursive algorithmic technique for solving constraint satisfaction problems. It incrementally builds candidates for a solution and abandons them as soon as it determines the candidate cannot possibly be completed to a valid solution. It is often used in problems like N-Queens, Sudoku, maze solving, and permutation generation. Backtracking can be visualized as a depth-first traversal of a state space tree. It is preferred when exhaustive search is needed with pruning possibilities to reduce unnecessary computations, leading to more efficient problem-solving in specific scenarios.

34. Explain the concept of memoization in dynamic programming.
Answer: Memoization is an optimization technique used in dynamic programming that stores the results of expensive function calls and reuses them when the same inputs occur again. It typically uses a hash table or array to cache results, reducing the time complexity of recursive solutions. Memoization transforms a recursive exponential-time algorithm into a polynomial-time one. It is used in problems like Fibonacci calculation, longest common subsequence, and knapsack problems. Unlike tabulation (bottom-up), memoization is a top-down approach, solving only the required subproblems and making recursive calls as needed.

35. What is a recurrence relation in algorithm analysis?
Answer: A recurrence relation expresses the running time of a recursive algorithm in terms of the running time of smaller inputs. It is used to analyze the time complexity of divide-and-conquer algorithms. For example, the recurrence for Merge Sort is $T(n) = 2T(n/2) + O(n)$, which solves to $O(n \log n)$. Solving recurrence relations helps determine the overall time complexity. Common techniques for solving them include the Master Theorem, recursion tree method, and substitution method. Understanding recurrence relations is essential for analyzing recursive algorithms.

36. How does the Master Theorem help in solving recurrence relations?
Answer: The Master Theorem provides a direct way to determine the time complexity of divide-and-conquer algorithms expressed by recurrence relations of the form $T(n) = aT(n/b) + f(n)$, where $a \geq 1$ and $b > 1$. It compares the

function f(n) with n^log_b(a) to determine whether the solution is polynomial, logarithmic, or linear. It classifies the time complexity into three cases, depending on the growth of f(n). The Master Theorem is widely used for algorithms like Merge Sort, Binary Search, and Strassen's Matrix Multiplication to derive asymptotic bounds easily.

37. What is the role of priority queues in algorithm design?
Answer: Priority queues are abstract data types where each element has a priority, and elements are dequeued in order of highest priority (typically using a min-heap or max-heap). They are crucial in algorithms like Dijkstra's shortest path, Prim's algorithm for MST, Huffman coding, and A* search. A binary heap is a common implementation, offering O(log n) insertion and deletion. Priority queues optimize greedy algorithms and help in managing dynamic datasets where quick access to the minimum or maximum element is needed. They enhance the performance of several classical algorithms.

38. Explain amortized analysis in algorithm performance.
Answer: Amortized analysis evaluates the average time per operation over a sequence of operations, ensuring that the worst-case cost of an individual operation does not overly affect the overall performance. It provides a more realistic performance measure than worst-case analysis. For example, in dynamic arrays, although resizing is expensive, it happens infrequently. Hence, the average cost per operation is low. Amortized analysis is used in data structures like splay trees, dynamic arrays, and Fibonacci heaps. It is calculated using methods like aggregate analysis, accounting method, and potential method.

39. What is a red-black tree and why is it used?
Answer: A red-black tree is a self-balancing binary search tree in which each node contains an extra bit for color (red or black). It maintains balance through specific rules during insertion and deletion, ensuring the tree height remains O(log n). This guarantees efficient search, insertion, and deletion operations. Red-black trees are used in implementations of associative containers like C++ STL's map and set, and Java's TreeMap. Their predictable performance and automatic balancing make them suitable for applications requiring ordered and balanced data access.

40. What are the advantages of using adjacency lists over adjacency matrices in graph representation?
Answer: Adjacency lists and matrices are two ways to represent graphs. Adjacency lists are more space-efficient for sparse graphs, using O(V + E) space, where V is the number of vertices and E is the number of edges. Adjacency matrices use $O(V^2)$ space regardless of edge count, making them inefficient for sparse graphs. Lists allow faster iteration over a vertex's neighbors, which is essential for traversal algorithms. However, matrices allow constant-time edge existence checks. The choice depends on graph density and the types of operations performed frequently.

41. What is the difference between Greedy algorithms and Dynamic Programming?
Answer: Greedy algorithms make the locally optimal choice at each step with the hope of finding a global optimum. They do not revisit choices, and hence, are faster but do not guarantee an optimal solution for all problems. Dynamic Programming, on the other hand, solves subproblems and stores their results to avoid recomputation. It ensures an optimal solution by considering all possible choices and using overlapping subproblems. Examples of Greedy include Prim's and Kruskal's algorithms, while DP examples are the Knapsack and Floyd-Warshall algorithms.

42. Explain Strassen's matrix multiplication algorithm.
Answer: Strassen's algorithm is a divide-and-conquer algorithm for matrix multiplication that reduces the number of recursive multiplications needed compared to the conventional method. For two n x n matrices, the traditional method performs $O(n^3)$ operations, whereas Strassen's reduces it to approximately O(n^2.81) by calculating 7 products instead of 8. It recursively divides matrices into submatrices and combines the results to form the final product. This technique is particularly efficient for large matrices and forms the basis of many fast matrix multiplication libraries.

43. What is the Rabin-Karp algorithm and how does it work?
Answer: The Rabin-Karp algorithm is a string-searching algorithm that uses hashing to find any one of a set of pattern strings in a text. It calculates a hash value for the pattern and for each substring of the text, comparing the hash values instead of individual characters. If a hash match is found, it performs a character-by-character comparison to confirm. It is efficient when searching for multiple patterns, achieving average-case time complexity of O(n + m) but can degrade to O(nm) in the worst case due to hash collisions.

44. Define the Floyd-Warshall algorithm and its application.
Answer: The Floyd-Warshall algorithm is a dynamic programming algorithm used to find the shortest paths between all pairs of vertices in a weighted graph. It works by considering all vertices as intermediate points and updating path lengths if a shorter path is found via an intermediate vertex. The algorithm works with both directed and undirected graphs and can handle negative weights but not negative cycles. It has a time complexity of $O(V^3)$ and is used in applications like network routing and transitive closure detection.

45. What is the use of graph coloring in algorithms?
Answer: Graph coloring involves assigning colors to the vertices of a graph such that no two adjacent vertices share the same color. It is used in various applications like scheduling, register allocation in compilers, and frequency assignment in cellular networks. The chromatic number is the minimum number of colors required to color a graph. Graph coloring problems are NP-complete, and heuristics or backtracking algorithms are used for practical solutions. Greedy algorithms can offer approximate results in linear time for certain graph types.

46. How does the topological sort work on Directed Acyclic Graphs (DAGs)?
Answer: Topological sorting is a linear ordering of vertices in a Directed Acyclic Graph (DAG) such that for every directed edge $u \rightarrow v$, vertex u appears before v in the ordering. It is useful in scheduling tasks, resolving symbol dependencies in compilers, and ordering cells in spreadsheet computations. It can be implemented using DFS (with a stack) or Kahn's algorithm (using in-degree counting and a queue). It only works on DAGs, and its time complexity is $O(V + E)$, where V and E are the number of vertices and edges, respectively.

47. What is NP-completeness in algorithm design?
Answer: NP-completeness refers to a class of problems for which no known polynomial-time solution exists, but for which a given solution can be verified in polynomial time. If one NP-complete problem is solved in polynomial time, then all NP problems can be solved in polynomial time. Common NP-complete problems include the Traveling Salesman Problem, 3-SAT, and Knapsack. Reductions are used to prove NP-completeness by transforming a known NP-complete problem into another in polynomial time. It plays a critical role in computational complexity theory and algorithm design.

48. Describe the concept of reduction in computational theory.
Answer: Reduction is a technique used to relate the complexity of two problems by transforming one problem into another. If problem A reduces to problem B, solving B allows us to solve A. It is used in proving NP-completeness, where a known NP-complete problem is reduced to another to show its hardness. Reductions must be performed in polynomial time. Types include polynomial-time reductions and many-one reductions. Reduction helps classify problems and determine whether a new problem is computationally feasible or intractable.

49. What is approximation algorithm and where is it used?
Answer: An approximation algorithm is used for NP-hard optimization problems where finding an exact solution is computationally infeasible. These algorithms provide solutions that are close to the optimal within a known bound. The performance is measured by the approximation ratio, which compares the algorithm's output to the optimal solution. They are widely used in problems like Vertex Cover, Traveling Salesman, and Set Cover. Approximation algorithms offer a trade-off between accuracy and computation time, making them valuable for real-world large-scale problems.

50. Explain the concept of randomized algorithms.
Answer: Randomized algorithms use random numbers during their logic to make decisions, which may influence their behavior and output. They are often simpler, faster, or more robust than deterministic algorithms. Types include Las Vegas algorithms (always correct, variable time) and Monte Carlo algorithms (bounded time, probabilistic correctness). Examples include Randomized QuickSort, Rabin-Karp, and randomized primality testing. These algorithms are used in cryptography, computer graphics, and numerical simulations. They provide average-case performance improvements and help avoid worst-case input scenarios.

51. What is the difference between deterministic and non-deterministic algorithms?
Answer: Deterministic algorithms operate in a predictable manner, producing the same output for a given input every time they run. They follow a specific sequence of steps and are easier to debug and analyze. Non-deterministic algorithms, on the other hand, can produce different outputs on different runs for the same input, as they may include

randomness or parallelism. In computational theory, non-determinism refers to the ability to explore multiple possibilities simultaneously. Non-deterministic algorithms are theoretical models often used to define classes like NP.

52. What is amortized time complexity and how is it calculated?

Answer: Amortized time complexity refers to the average time per operation over a sequence of operations, accounting for both cheap and expensive operations. It is used when a data structure occasionally performs a costly operation that compensates for many cheaper ones. For example, dynamic array resizing is expensive, but happens infrequently, leading to an overall low average cost per insertion. Amortized analysis techniques include the aggregate method, the accounting method, and the potential method. It gives a more realistic understanding of algorithm performance over time.

53. Explain the significance of hashing in algorithm design.

Answer: Hashing is a technique used to map data of arbitrary size to fixed-size values, typically for fast data retrieval. It is fundamental in creating efficient data structures like hash tables, sets, and maps. Hashing allows average-case O(1) access time, making it ideal for lookup-intensive applications. The efficiency of hashing depends on a good hash function and collision resolution strategy (like chaining or open addressing). Hashing is widely used in databases, compilers, caching, and cryptographic applications for ensuring data integrity and quick access.

54. What are the different types of tree traversal methods?

Answer: Tree traversal methods include:

Inorder Traversal – Visits left subtree, root, then right subtree (used in BSTs for sorted output).

Preorder Traversal – Visits root, then left and right subtrees (used in copying trees).

Postorder Traversal – Visits left and right subtrees, then root (used in deleting trees).

Level Order Traversal – Visits nodes level by level using a queue.

These methods are implemented using recursion or iteration and serve different use cases in data manipulation and expression parsing.

55. How do splay trees work and where are they used?

Answer: Splay trees are self-adjusting binary search trees that move recently accessed elements to the root using rotations. This operation is called "splaying" and helps keep frequently accessed elements near the top, improving access time for those elements. Although individual operations can take O(n) time, the amortized time is O(log n). Splay trees are used in caches, garbage collectors, and network routers where temporal locality of reference is common. Their simplicity and good average-case performance make them practical alternatives to balanced trees.

56. What is a suffix tree and its application?

Answer: A suffix tree is a compressed trie that represents all suffixes of a given string. It allows linear-time string operations such as substring search, pattern matching, and longest repeated substring finding. It is constructed in O(n) time using algorithms like Ukkonen's algorithm. Suffix trees are used in bioinformatics for DNA sequence analysis, data compression, and search engines. They provide efficient solutions to complex string problems that would otherwise require quadratic time using naive approaches.

57. What is the complexity of QuickSort in best, average, and worst cases?

Answer: The time complexities of QuickSort are:

Best Case: O(n log n), occurs when the pivot divides the array evenly.

Average Case: O(n log n), assuming random pivot choices.

Worst Case: O(n^2), happens when the pivot is the smallest or largest element repeatedly.

Despite its worst-case complexity, QuickSort is widely used due to its average performance and cache efficiency. Randomized pivot selection helps mitigate the worst-case scenario.

58. What are the properties of AVL trees?

Answer: AVL trees are self-balancing binary search trees where the height difference (balance factor) between the left and right subtrees of any node is at most one. They ensure O(log n) time for search, insertion, and deletion by performing rotations (single and double) to maintain balance. AVL trees are stricter than Red-Black trees in balancing, which leads to faster lookups but more rotations. They are used in applications requiring frequent search operations with ordered data, such as databases and memory indexing.

59. What is a B-Tree and how is it used in databases?
Answer: A B-Tree is a self-balancing tree data structure that maintains sorted data and allows searches, sequential access, insertions, and deletions in logarithmic time. Unlike binary search trees, B-Trees can have multiple children, making them suitable for disk-based storage. They minimize disk reads and are optimized for systems that read and write large blocks of data. B-Trees are widely used in databases and file systems (e.g., NTFS, HFS) where quick access to large data is essential. They are the basis for B+ Trees, which further optimize range queries.

60. What is a minimum spanning tree (MST) and how is it computed?
Answer: A minimum spanning tree (MST) is a subset of the edges of a connected, weighted, undirected graph that connects all vertices with the minimum possible total edge weight and without any cycles. MSTs are used in network design, clustering, and approximation algorithms. Common algorithms to compute MST include:
Kruskal's Algorithm: Adds edges in increasing order of weight, using union-find to detect cycles.
Prim's Algorithm: Grows the MST by adding the minimum weight edge from the tree to a new vertex.
Both algorithms run in O(E log V) time using appropriate data structures.

61. What is memoization in dynamic programming?
Answer: Memoization is a technique used to optimize recursive algorithms by storing the results of expensive function calls and reusing them when the same inputs occur again. It is a top-down approach in dynamic programming where function values are cached after their initial computation. This avoids redundant calculations, reduces time complexity, and enhances efficiency. Memoization is especially useful in problems like Fibonacci computation, shortest paths, and parsing where overlapping subproblems are common. It is typically implemented using arrays or hash maps.

62. Explain the Longest Common Subsequence (LCS) problem.
Answer: The Longest Common Subsequence (LCS) problem involves finding the longest sequence that appears in the same relative order in two given sequences but not necessarily contiguously. It is solved using dynamic programming by building a 2D table that records the length of LCS at each point. The time and space complexity is O(m*n) where m and n are lengths of the input sequences. LCS is used in version control, bioinformatics, and diff tools to identify similarities and differences between strings.

63. What is the difference between LCS and Longest Common Substring?
Answer: LCS (Longest Common Subsequence) finds the longest sequence of characters that appear in both strings in the same order but not necessarily contiguously. In contrast, the Longest Common Substring requires the characters to be consecutive in both strings. LCS allows more flexibility, making it suitable for comparison tools and DNA sequencing, whereas the substring problem is used in plagiarism detection and text processing. LCS is solved using dynamic programming with a full table, while substring problems often use diagonal checks or suffix trees.

64. What is tail recursion and why is it important?
Answer: Tail recursion is a type of recursion where the recursive call is the last operation in the function. It allows compilers to optimize the call stack by reusing stack frames, making recursion as memory-efficient as iteration. This optimization is known as tail call optimization (TCO). Tail recursion is important in functional programming and languages that support TCO, as it allows writing recursive solutions without the risk of stack overflow. It improves performance and is used in problems like factorial calculation and list processing.

65. What is a binary heap and its applications?
Answer: A binary heap is a complete binary tree that satisfies the heap property — for a max-heap, the parent is greater than or equal to its children; for a min-heap, the parent is smaller. Binary heaps are implemented using arrays and support efficient insertion and extraction operations in O(log n) time. They are used in priority queues, heap sort, and graph algorithms like Dijkstra's and Prim's. Their structure ensures quick access to the highest or lowest priority element.

66. Describe the working of heap sort.
Answer: Heap sort is a comparison-based sorting algorithm that uses a binary heap to sort elements. It first builds a max-heap from the input data, ensuring the largest element is at the root. Then, it repeatedly swaps the root with the last element, reduces the heap size, and heapifies the new root. This process continues until the array is sorted. Heap sort has O(n log n) time complexity in all cases and is an in-place algorithm, but it is not stable.

67. What is the difference between divide and conquer and dynamic programming?
Answer: Both are algorithm design paradigms, but they differ in approach. Divide and Conquer breaks a problem into independent subproblems, solves them recursively, and combines their results. Dynamic Programming breaks a problem into overlapping subproblems, solves each once, and stores their solutions for reuse. While Divide and Conquer is used in algorithms like Merge Sort and QuickSort, Dynamic Programming is used in problems like Knapsack and Matrix Chain Multiplication. The key difference is that DP avoids recomputation through memorization.

68. What are articulation points in a graph?
Answer: An articulation point (or cut vertex) in a graph is a vertex that, if removed along with its edges, increases the number of connected components. These points are critical for network reliability and vulnerability analysis. They are found using depth-first search (DFS) by tracking discovery and low times. Applications include identifying network bottlenecks and designing fault-tolerant systems. In a DFS tree, a node is an articulation point if (a) it's the root with multiple children, or (b) any child cannot reach an ancestor of the node.

69. What is the role of backtracking in algorithm design?
Answer: Backtracking is a general algorithmic technique for solving recursive problems by trying out possible solutions and abandoning them if they do not satisfy the problem constraints. It is used in constraint satisfaction problems such as Sudoku, N-Queens, and combinatorial generation. Backtracking explores the solution space in a depth-first manner and uses pruning to avoid unnecessary work. Although it may have exponential time complexity in the worst case, it is practical for many problems due to its ability to eliminate large parts of the search space.

70. Describe the branch and bound technique.
Answer: Branch and Bound is a problem-solving technique used for optimization problems, especially those involving combinatorial search. It systematically explores the solution space by branching into subproblems and bounding regions that cannot yield better solutions than already found ones. It is widely used in solving problems like the Traveling Salesman, Integer Programming, and Knapsack. Unlike backtracking, which only checks for feasibility, Branch and Bound also maintains the best solution found and prunes branches using upper and lower bounds.

71. What is time complexity and how is it measured?
Answer: Time complexity measures the amount of time an algorithm takes to complete as a function of input size. It is expressed using Big O notation to describe the upper bound of growth. For instance, O(1) denotes constant time, O(log n) logarithmic, O(n) linear, O(n log n) logarithmic-linear, and $O(n^2)$ quadratic time. Time complexity helps in comparing algorithm efficiency and scalability. It is measured through step counting, experimental profiling, or using recurrence relations for recursive algorithms.

72. Explain the Bellman-Ford algorithm.
Answer: The Bellman-Ford algorithm computes the shortest paths from a single source to all other vertices in a weighted graph, including graphs with negative edge weights. It relaxes all edges repeatedly for V-1 times, where V is the number of vertices. If a shorter path is found in the V-th iteration, it indicates a negative weight cycle. Bellman-Ford has a time complexity of O(VE) and is useful where Dijkstra's algorithm fails due to negative weights, such as in currency arbitrage and routing protocols.

73. What is an Eulerian path and how do you find it?
Answer: An Eulerian path in a graph is a trail that visits every edge exactly once. An Eulerian circuit is an Eulerian path that starts and ends at the same vertex. For an undirected graph to have an Eulerian path, it must be connected and have exactly 0 or 2 vertices of odd degree. Fleury's algorithm and Hierholzer's algorithm are commonly used to find Eulerian paths. Applications include DNA sequencing and network optimization.

74. What is the purpose of Kruskal's algorithm?
Answer: Kruskal's algorithm is a greedy algorithm used to find the Minimum Spanning Tree (MST) of a graph. It sorts all the edges by weight and adds them one by one to the MST, provided they do not form a cycle. A disjoint-set (union-find) data structure is used to detect cycles efficiently. The algorithm ensures a globally optimal solution by always choosing the next minimum weight edge. Its time complexity is O(E log E), where E is the number of edges.

75. How does Dijkstra's algorithm work and when is it used?
Answer: Dijkstra's algorithm finds the shortest path from a source vertex to all other vertices in a graph with non-negative edge weights. It uses a priority queue to always pick the vertex with the smallest tentative distance. The distances are updated as shorter paths are found. It has a time complexity of $O(V^2)$ for a basic implementation and $O((V + E) \log V)$ with a binary heap. It is used in GPS systems, routing, and network pathfinding where edge weights are non-negative.

76. What is a Hamiltonian path and how is it different from Eulerian path?
Answer: A Hamiltonian path in a graph is a path that visits each vertex exactly once. Unlike an Eulerian path, which concerns edges and requires each edge to be visited exactly once, the Hamiltonian path focuses on visiting all vertices once. Determining whether such a path exists is NP-complete, and there is no efficient known algorithm to solve it for all cases. It is useful in problems like the Traveling Salesman Problem and various scheduling applications.

77. Explain the concept of amortized analysis.
Answer: Amortized analysis provides the average time per operation over a sequence of operations, guaranteeing that the average performance remains within a bound even if individual operations might be costly. It differs from average-case analysis by assuming worst-case input but spreading the cost across multiple operations. It is used in data structures like dynamic arrays, splay trees, and Fibonacci heaps, where occasional costly operations are offset by many inexpensive ones.

78. What is the pigeonhole principle and how is it used in algorithms?
Answer: The pigeonhole principle states that if more items are put into fewer containers than the number of items, at least one container must contain more than one item. In algorithms, it is used to prove the existence of certain properties, such as in hashing collisions, birthday paradox, and space-efficient algorithms. It is also used in theoretical proofs involving combinatorics, graph coloring, and distribution problems.

79. What are approximation algorithms?
Answer: Approximation algorithms are algorithms designed for NP-hard optimization problems where finding an exact solution is computationally infeasible. These algorithms provide solutions close to the optimal within a guaranteed factor, called the approximation ratio. For example, the Vertex Cover problem has a 2-approximation algorithm. These are crucial in real-world applications where performance or response time is more important than absolute accuracy.

80. Explain primality testing algorithms.
Answer: Primality testing algorithms determine whether a number is prime. Simple methods include trial division and Sieve of Eratosthenes. More advanced methods include the Fermat test, Miller-Rabin probabilistic test, and the AKS primality test which is deterministic and runs in polynomial time. These algorithms are vital in cryptography, especially in public-key algorithms like RSA that require large prime numbers for secure encryption.

81. What is the Max-Flow Min-Cut theorem?
Answer: The Max-Flow Min-Cut theorem states that in a flow network, the maximum amount of flow from the source to the sink is equal to the minimum capacity that, when removed, would disconnect the source from the sink. This theorem is foundational in network flow algorithms and is applied using algorithms like Ford-Fulkerson and Edmonds-Karp. It has practical applications in transportation, logistics, and network bandwidth optimization.

82. What is the difference between top-down and bottom-up dynamic programming?
Answer: Top-down dynamic programming, also known as memoization, involves solving the problem recursively and storing results of subproblems to avoid redundant computations. Bottom-up, or tabulation, solves smaller subproblems first and uses their results to build up solutions to larger problems iteratively. Bottom-up is often more space- and time-efficient due to reduced overhead from recursive calls and better cache locality.

83. Explain the use of Fibonacci heaps in algorithms.
Answer: Fibonacci heaps are advanced data structures used to implement priority queues with better amortized time complexities than binary heaps. They support operations like insert, decrease-key, and merge in constant amortized time, making them suitable for graph algorithms like Dijkstra's and Prim's when used with a large number of nodes and edges. Their complex structure includes a collection of heap-ordered trees with pointers for efficient updates.

84. What is the significance of the Master Theorem in algorithm analysis?
Answer: The Master Theorem provides a method to determine the time complexity of divide-and-conquer algorithms. It offers a formulaic approach to solving recurrence relations of the form $T(n) = aT(n/b) + f(n)$, where $a \geq 1$, $b > 1$, and $f(n)$ is an additional cost. By comparing $f(n)$ with n^log_b(a), it categorizes the complexity into cases. This theorem is widely used in analyzing algorithms like Merge Sort, Binary Search, and Strassen's matrix multiplication.

85. What are randomized algorithms and when are they used?
Answer: Randomized algorithms use random numbers to influence their behavior and decision-making during execution. They can provide performance guarantees with high probability or simplify complex deterministic solutions. Examples include Randomized QuickSort, Monte Carlo algorithms, and Las Vegas algorithms. They are used in cryptography, load balancing, and computational geometry where randomness improves performance or ensures fairness.

86. Describe the Rabin-Karp string matching algorithm.
Answer: The Rabin-Karp algorithm uses hashing to find a pattern in a text efficiently. It calculates the hash value of the pattern and compares it with the hash values of substrings of the text. If a match is found, it verifies the actual characters to confirm the match. It achieves average-case time complexity of $O(n + m)$ but can degrade to $O(nm)$ in the worst case due to hash collisions. It is particularly effective for detecting multiple patterns simultaneously.

87. What is the role of hashing in algorithm design?
Answer: Hashing is used to map data to a fixed-size value (hash code) that allows quick data access, insertion, and deletion. In algorithm design, it supports constant-time complexity operations in hash tables, used in data structures like sets, maps, and caches. Hashing is fundamental in algorithms for duplicate detection, string matching, and cryptographic applications. Good hash functions minimize collisions and distribute data uniformly.

88. What are the different types of graph representations?
Answer: Graphs can be represented in several ways:
Adjacency Matrix – a 2D array indicating edge presence; space complexity is $O(V^2)$.
Adjacency List – lists for each vertex containing its neighbors; space complexity is $O(V + E)$.
Edge List – a list of all edges as pairs of vertices.
Each has advantages depending on the graph's density and the type of operations required.

89. What is a B-tree and where is it used?
Answer: A B-tree is a self-balancing tree data structure used for storing sorted data and allowing searches, insertions, and deletions in logarithmic time. Unlike binary trees, B-trees can have more than two children and are optimized for systems that read and write large blocks of data. They are commonly used in databases and file systems, such as in indexing and managing disk-based storage.

90. What is the Floyd-Warshall algorithm used for?
Answer: The Floyd-Warshall algorithm computes the shortest paths between all pairs of vertices in a weighted graph. It uses dynamic programming to update a distance matrix, considering all possible intermediate vertices. Its time complexity is $O(V^3)$, making it suitable for small to medium-sized dense graphs. It can also detect negative cycles and is used in routing and network optimization.

91. What is a suffix tree and its applications?
Answer: A suffix tree is a compressed trie of all the suffixes of a string. It allows efficient string matching, substring search, and pattern matching in linear time. Applications include bioinformatics (DNA analysis), data compression, plagiarism detection, and search engines. Constructing a suffix tree takes $O(n)$ time and space, and it enables solving many string problems efficiently.

92. What is the difference between NP, NP-hard, and NP-complete problems?
Answer: NP (nondeterministic polynomial time) problems are those verifiable in polynomial time. NP-hard problems are at least as hard as the hardest problems in NP but may not be in NP themselves. NP-complete problems are both in NP and NP-hard. Solving one NP-complete problem in polynomial time implies all NP problems can be solved in polynomial time. Understanding these classes helps in identifying computational feasibility.

93. What is a greedy algorithm and give a real-world example?
Answer: A greedy algorithm makes the locally optimal choice at each step with the hope of finding a global optimum. It is simple and efficient but does not always guarantee the best solution. Real-world examples include coin change (with standard denominations), Kruskal's MST algorithm, and Huffman coding for data compression. Greedy strategies are effective when the problem exhibits the greedy-choice property and optimal substructure.

94. What is the clique problem in graph theory?
Answer: The clique problem involves finding a complete subgraph (clique) in a given graph, where every pair of vertices is connected. The maximum clique problem, which asks for the largest such subgraph, is NP-complete. It has applications in social network analysis, bioinformatics, and computational chemistry. Due to its complexity, approximation and heuristic algorithms are often used in practice.

95. How does the QuickSelect algorithm work?
Answer: QuickSelect is an algorithm to find the k-th smallest element in an unordered list. It is based on the partitioning logic of QuickSort but only recurses into one partition, depending on the position of the pivot. Its average time complexity is O(n), but the worst case is $O(n^2)$. QuickSelect is efficient for problems requiring order statistics like median finding or percentile calculations.

96. What is the significance of the Bellman-Ford algorithm in graph theory?
Answer: The Bellman-Ford algorithm is used to compute shortest paths from a single source vertex to all other vertices in a weighted graph, even when some of the edge weights are negative. Unlike Dijkstra's algorithm, Bellman-Ford can handle graphs with negative weight edges, and it can also detect negative weight cycles. It works by relaxing all edges repeatedly and has a time complexity of O(VE), making it suitable for sparse graphs.

97. What is a red-black tree?
Answer: A red-black tree is a self-balancing binary search tree where each node contains an extra bit for denoting the color of the node, either red or black. The tree maintains balance using five properties that enforce rules about how red and black nodes can appear in relation to one another. These properties ensure that the longest path from the root to any leaf is no more than twice as long as the shortest path, maintaining O(log n) time for insertion, deletion, and lookup operations.

98. Describe the role of dynamic programming in solving the Longest Common Subsequence (LCS) problem.
Answer: Dynamic programming is ideal for solving the LCS problem because it breaks the problem into smaller overlapping subproblems and stores the solutions in a table to avoid redundant computations. The LCS algorithm uses a 2D matrix to track matches between characters in two sequences and builds up the length of the longest common subsequence in a bottom-up manner. It has a time complexity of O(mn), where m and n are the lengths of the two sequences.

99. What is a spanning tree and how does it differ from a minimum spanning tree?
Answer: A spanning tree of a connected graph is a subset of the edges that connects all the vertices without forming any cycles. A minimum spanning tree (MST) is a spanning tree with the minimum total edge weight. While any connected graph can have multiple spanning trees, the MST is unique (in the case of distinct edge weights) and is used in network design, clustering, and circuit design.

100. How does backtracking work and where is it used?
Answer: Backtracking is a recursive algorithmic technique for solving problems incrementally, trying partial solutions and abandoning them if they fail to satisfy the constraints. It is used in problems that require searching through all possible combinations, such as N-Queens, Sudoku, and the Knapsack problem. Backtracking reduces the number of possibilities to consider by pruning invalid solutions early, but its worst-case time complexity can still be exponential.

101. What is the concept of memoization in dynamic programming?
Answer: Memoization is a top-down approach in dynamic programming where results of expensive function calls are stored and reused when the same inputs occur again. It combines recursion with caching and helps in improving performance by avoiding repeated computations. Unlike tabulation, which is bottom-up, memoization starts from the

original problem and works its way down, only computing necessary subproblems. It is particularly useful for problems with overlapping subproblems and optimal substructure.

102. Explain the relationship between P, NP, and NP-complete problems.
Answer: P is the set of problems that can be solved in polynomial time. NP is the set of problems for which solutions can be verified in polynomial time. NP-complete problems are those that are both in NP and as hard as any problem in NP. If any NP-complete problem can be solved in polynomial time, then all NP problems can be solved in polynomial time (i.e., P = NP). This is a fundamental question in theoretical computer science.

103. What are decision trees in the context of algorithm analysis?
Answer: Decision trees in algorithm analysis are used to model the decision-making process of algorithms, especially in comparison-based sorting. The tree represents all possible sequences of comparisons made by the algorithm. The height of the decision tree gives a lower bound on the number of comparisons needed in the worst case. For example, the lower bound for comparison-based sorting is $\Omega(n \log n)$, as derived using decision tree analysis.

104. Describe the use of tries in string algorithms.
Answer: A trie, or prefix tree, is a tree-like data structure that stores a dynamic set of strings where the keys are usually strings. It enables efficient search, insert, and delete operations with time complexity proportional to the length of the word. Tries are widely used in autocomplete systems, spell checkers, and IP routing. They also support longest prefix matching and can be space-optimized using techniques like compressed tries or radix trees.

105. What is the purpose of bit manipulation in algorithm design?
Answer: Bit manipulation involves using bitwise operations like AND, OR, XOR, and shifts to perform computations at the binary level. It is used to optimize performance, reduce memory usage, and simplify complex logic. Common uses include checking for even/odd numbers, swapping values without temporary variables, and implementing efficient algorithms in cryptography, hashing, and graphics. Bit tricks are crucial in low-level programming and competitive coding.

106. How does the union-find data structure work?
Answer: The union-find (or disjoint-set) data structure keeps track of a partition of a set into disjoint subsets and supports two main operations: find, which identifies the set a particular element belongs to, and union, which merges two subsets. It is used in Kruskal's algorithm and in applications like network connectivity and image processing. Path compression and union by rank optimizations make both operations nearly constant time, amortized.

107. What is the complexity class co-NP?
Answer: The complexity class co-NP consists of decision problems whose complements are in NP. That means for a problem in co-NP, a "no" answer can be verified in polynomial time. While NP deals with problems where "yes" instances are verifiable efficiently, co-NP focuses on "no" instances. Whether NP equals co-NP is an open question, similar to the P vs. NP problem, and resolving it would have profound implications in theoretical computer science.

108. What is the concept of recursion tree method?
Answer: The recursion tree method is a visual tool to solve recurrence relations by representing the recursive calls of an algorithm as a tree. It helps estimate the total work done by summing the work at each level. This method is especially useful when applying the Master Theorem is not straightforward. It is commonly used in analyzing divide-and-conquer algorithms like Merge Sort, QuickSort, and binary tree traversals.

109. What is alpha-beta pruning in game tree algorithms?
Answer: Alpha-beta pruning is an optimization technique for the minimax algorithm in game trees. It eliminates branches that won't affect the final decision, thus reducing the number of nodes evaluated. The alpha value represents the best already explored option along the path to the root for the maximizer, and beta for the minimizer. Pruning improves efficiency without affecting the correctness, making it essential for games like chess or tic-tac-toe.

110. What are the applications of linear programming in algorithms?
Answer: Linear programming (LP) involves optimizing a linear objective function subject to linear constraints. In algorithm design, LP is used for problems like resource allocation, scheduling, and network flow. Algorithms like the

Simplex method and interior point methods solve LP problems efficiently. LP is also applied in operations research, economics, and computational biology for modeling and optimizing real-world systems.

111. What is the role of divide-and-conquer in matrix multiplication?
Answer: Divide-and-conquer algorithms like Strassen's algorithm are used to speed up matrix multiplication by dividing large matrices into smaller submatrices. This reduces the overall number of multiplications from the naive $O(n^3)$ to approximately O(n^2.81). Further improvements with algorithms like Coppersmith-Winograd aim to reduce this further. These methods are foundational in scientific computing, computer graphics, and numerical simulations.

112. Explain the Chinese Remainder Theorem and its algorithmic significance.
Answer: The Chinese Remainder Theorem states that if one knows the remainders of the division of an integer by several pairwise coprime integers, then there is a unique integer solution modulo the product of those integers. It is used in cryptography, particularly RSA encryption, and modular arithmetic algorithms. Its algorithmic implementation allows efficient computations over large numbers, often improving performance significantly.

113. What is the difference between deterministic and non-deterministic algorithms?
Answer: Deterministic algorithms produce the same output for a given input every time and follow a fixed sequence of operations. Non-deterministic algorithms can have different outcomes on different executions with the same input, often modeled using randomness or guessing. While real computers are deterministic, non-determinism is used in theoretical models like NP problems and is central to understanding computational complexity.

114. What is memoization versus caching?
Answer: Memoization is a specific form of caching used in dynamic programming where results of expensive function calls are stored to avoid redundant computation. Caching, more broadly, refers to storing frequently accessed data or computations, often in a separate hardware or memory layer to improve performance. Memoization typically occurs at the software level in recursive algorithms, while caching can be hardware-assisted and system-wide.

115. How do bloom filters work in algorithmic design?
Answer: Bloom filters are probabilistic data structures used to test whether an element is a member of a set. They allow for false positives but not false negatives. A bloom filter uses multiple hash functions to set bits in a bit array; when checking for membership, all relevant bits must be set. They are space-efficient and used in databases, web caches, and spam filters for quick membership testing.

116. What is tail recursion and how is it optimized?
Answer: Tail recursion occurs when a function makes a recursive call as its final operation. It can be optimized by the compiler into an iterative loop, saving stack space and preventing stack overflow. Languages like Scheme and modern compilers for C or Python support tail call optimization under certain conditions. Tail recursion is preferred when designing recursive algorithms that need to be memory-efficient.

117. Explain the concept of potential method in amortized analysis.
Answer: The potential method assigns a potential value to the data structure representing its stored "energy" or future work. The amortized cost of an operation is calculated as the actual cost plus the change in potential. This technique helps analyze sequences of operations more accurately, especially for dynamic structures like splay trees or Fibonacci heaps, where costly operations are infrequent but impactful.

118. What is a linear-time selection algorithm?
Answer: A linear-time selection algorithm finds the k-th smallest element in an unsorted list in O(n) time. The Median of Medians algorithm is a classic example that guarantees linear time by choosing a good pivot. This is important for order-statistics and is used in problems like finding the median, statistical sampling, and real-time data stream processing.

119. What is the time complexity of different graph traversal algorithms?
Answer: Both Breadth-First Search (BFS) and Depth-First Search (DFS) have a time complexity of O(V + E), where V is the number of vertices and E is the number of edges. They visit every node and edge once and are foundational for pathfinding, component detection, and graph analysis. Their efficiency depends on the graph's density and representation (adjacency list or matrix).

120. What are the types of recursion?
Answer: Types of recursion include:
Tail recursion – recursive call is the last action.
Head recursion – recursive call happens before processing.
Tree recursion – multiple recursive calls per function.
Indirect recursion – a function calls another which eventually calls the original.
Each type affects the algorithm's call stack behavior and optimization possibilities.

121. How is Euclid's algorithm used to compute GCD?
Answer: Euclid's algorithm efficiently computes the greatest common divisor (GCD) of two integers by repeatedly applying the operation GCD(a, b) = GCD(b, a % b) until b becomes zero. It has a time complexity of O(log min(a, b)) and is used in cryptography, number theory, and simplifying fractions. It is one of the oldest known algorithms and remains highly efficient and relevant.

122. What is the difference between an AVL tree and a Red-Black tree?
Answer: AVL trees are more rigidly balanced than Red-Black trees, ensuring that the heights of subtrees differ by at most one. This results in faster lookups but more rotations during insertions and deletions. Red-Black trees allow a looser balance with fewer rotations, leading to better performance in frequent updates. The choice depends on the application: AVL for faster search; Red-Black for frequent modifications.

123. What is a heap and how is it used in algorithms?
Answer: A heap is a complete binary tree that satisfies the heap property: the key at the root must be minimum (min-heap) or maximum (max-heap) among all nodes. It supports efficient insert and extract-min/max operations in O(log n) time. Heaps are used in priority queues, heap sort, and graph algorithms like Dijkstra's. Binary, binomial, and Fibonacci heaps offer different trade-offs for operations.

124. What is iterative deepening search (IDS)?
Answer: IDS is a search algorithm that combines the space-efficiency of DFS with the optimality of BFS. It performs DFS with increasing depth limits until a solution is found. It is useful in scenarios like game tree exploration where the search depth is unknown. Though it appears redundant, its performance is similar to BFS with significantly reduced memory usage.

125. What is the difference between divide-and-conquer and dynamic programming?
Answer: Both divide-and-conquer and dynamic programming solve problems by breaking them into subproblems. The key difference is that dynamic programming solves overlapping subproblems and stores their results (memoization or tabulation), while divide-and-conquer solves independent subproblems without storing results. Merge Sort is an example of divide-and-conquer, while Fibonacci computation using memoization is dynamic programming. Choosing the right approach depends on the problem's structure.

Chapter 7: Most Asked Questions Part-B

1. What is a randomized algorithm, and how does it differ from deterministic algorithms?
Answer: A randomized algorithm uses random numbers to influence its decisions during execution. Unlike deterministic algorithms, which produce the same output for a given input every time, randomized algorithms may yield different results or execution paths for the same input. They are particularly useful for problems where a deterministic solution is too slow or difficult to implement efficiently. Randomized algorithms are categorized into two types: Las Vegas algorithms, which always produce the correct result but have variable runtimes, and Monte Carlo algorithms, which may produce incorrect results with a small probability. These algorithms are widely used in cryptography, primality testing, and optimization problems.

2. What is the Master Theorem, and how is it used in algorithm analysis?
Answer: The Master Theorem provides a way to analyze the time complexity of divide-and-conquer algorithms without solving recurrence relations manually. It applies to recurrence relations of the form $T(n) = aT(n/b) + f(n)$, where $a \geq 1$, $b > 1$, and $f(n)$ is an asymptotically positive function. The theorem offers three cases based on the growth rate of f(n) compared to n^log_b(a). Each case determines whether the recursive part, the non-recursive work, or both contribute dominantly to the time complexity. It simplifies the complexity analysis of algorithms such as mergesort and quicksort, making it a vital tool in algorithm design.

3. What are approximation algorithms, and when are they used?
Answer: Approximation algorithms are used to find near-optimal solutions for optimization problems that are NP-hard, where finding the exact solution is computationally infeasible. These algorithms are designed to run in polynomial time and produce solutions within a known bound of the optimal. They are commonly applied in problems like the traveling salesman problem, vertex cover, and knapsack problem. The quality of an approximation algorithm is measured by its approximation ratio, which compares the algorithm's output with the optimal solution. Approximation algorithms are crucial for decision-making in scenarios where time and resources are limited, and exact solutions are not practical.

4. What is dynamic programming, and how does it differ from divide-and-conquer?
Answer: Dynamic programming (DP) is an algorithmic technique used to solve problems by breaking them into overlapping subproblems, solving each subproblem once, and storing the results for future use. This avoids redundant calculations and improves efficiency. In contrast, divide-and-conquer breaks problems into independent subproblems, solves them recursively, and combines the results. While both strategies involve problem decomposition, DP is specifically used when subproblems recur multiple times. It is typically implemented in two ways: top-down (memoization) and bottom-up (tabulation). DP is ideal for optimization problems such as the knapsack problem, matrix chain multiplication, and shortest path computations like Floyd-Warshall.

5. What is amortized analysis, and why is it important?
Answer: Amortized analysis is a method used to average the time required to perform a sequence of operations over all the operations, ensuring that occasional expensive operations do not skew the average performance. Unlike worst-case analysis, which considers the maximum time for any single operation, amortized analysis provides a more realistic view of an algorithm's efficiency across multiple operations. It is particularly useful in data structures where most operations are fast, but some are costly, like dynamic arrays, splay trees, and Fibonacci heaps. By analyzing total cost over n operations, it helps in choosing more efficient algorithms in practical scenarios.

6. What is the significance of Big-O notation in algorithm analysis?
Answer: Big-O notation describes the upper bound of an algorithm's running time or space requirement in terms of input size, giving a high-level understanding of its performance. It helps compare algorithms based on their scalability and efficiency, abstracting away hardware or implementation-specific details. Big-O focuses on the worst-case scenario, ensuring performance expectations even in the most demanding cases. It is essential for predicting how algorithms behave as input sizes grow, influencing algorithm choice and system design. Common Big-O complexities include O(1), O(log n), O(n), O(n log n), $O(n^2)$, and exponential time complexities like O(2^n).

7. What is a recurrence relation in the context of algorithm analysis?
Answer: A recurrence relation is a mathematical expression that defines a function or sequence in terms of its values

at smaller inputs. In algorithm analysis, recurrence relations are used to describe the running time of recursive algorithms. For instance, mergesort's time complexity is defined by $T(n) = 2T(n/2) + O(n)$. Solving these relations provides insight into the overall time complexity of the algorithm. Common methods for solving recurrence relations include the Master Theorem, substitution method, and recursion tree method. Understanding and solving recurrence relations is crucial for accurately analyzing the performance of divide-and-conquer algorithms.

8. What is tail recursion, and how is it optimized in algorithm implementation?
Answer: Tail recursion is a special type of recursion where the recursive call is the last operation in the function. In tail-recursive functions, there is no need to keep the current function's state after the recursive call returns, which allows some compilers or interpreters to optimize it into a loop, reducing the call stack size. This optimization is known as tail call optimization (TCO), and it prevents stack overflow errors in deep recursions. Tail recursion is particularly useful in functional programming and is commonly applied in problems involving iteration, such as computing factorials or traversing lists.

9. What is backtracking, and how is it applied in algorithms?
Answer: Backtracking is an algorithmic paradigm used for solving problems incrementally by trying partial solutions and then abandoning them if they do not lead to a complete solution. It is often used for problems involving permutations, combinations, or constraint satisfaction. Classic applications include solving puzzles like Sudoku, the N-Queens problem, and generating subsets or permutations. Backtracking systematically explores all possible configurations and uses pruning to discard unviable options, making it efficient in practice for many combinatorial problems. It is typically implemented using recursion and is closely related to depth-first search in graphs and trees.

10. What are greedy algorithms, and in which scenarios are they most effective?
Answer: Greedy algorithms build up a solution piece by piece, always choosing the locally optimal option at each step with the hope of finding a global optimum. They are efficient and easy to implement but do not guarantee optimal solutions for all problems. Greedy algorithms work best in problems that exhibit the greedy-choice property and optimal substructure. Classic examples include Kruskal's and Prim's algorithms for minimum spanning trees, Dijkstra's algorithm for shortest paths, and the activity selection problem. Their effectiveness depends on the problem structure, and correctness often requires a formal proof that the greedy choice leads to an optimal solution.

11. What is memoization, and how does it differ from dynamic programming?
Answer: Memoization is a technique used to speed up recursive algorithms by storing the results of expensive function calls and returning the cached result when the same inputs occur again. It is a top-down approach in dynamic programming, where the function calls itself recursively and caches intermediate results. In contrast, the bottom-up approach of dynamic programming involves solving all subproblems iteratively and building up the final solution. While both techniques aim to avoid redundant computations, memoization is often easier to implement with recursion but can be less efficient in terms of space compared to tabulation used in bottom-up DP.

12. What is the significance of graph algorithms in computer science?
Answer: Graph algorithms are fundamental in computer science as they provide solutions for various problems involving networks, relationships, and dependencies. Applications include shortest path finding (e.g., Dijkstra's algorithm), minimum spanning trees (e.g., Prim's and Kruskal's algorithms), graph traversal (DFS, BFS), and cycle detection. They are widely used in networking, social media analysis, web search engines, compiler optimization, and logistics. Understanding graph algorithms is crucial for designing systems that require data modeling with nodes and edges, enabling the development of efficient and scalable software solutions in numerous domains.

13. What is the difference between DFS and BFS in graph traversal?
Answer: Depth-First Search (DFS) explores a graph by going as deep as possible along each branch before backtracking, using a stack data structure (either explicitly or via recursion). It is useful for problems like pathfinding, topological sorting, and detecting cycles. Breadth-First Search (BFS), on the other hand, explores the graph level by level using a queue. It is ideal for finding the shortest path in unweighted graphs and checking bipartiteness. The main difference lies in their traversal strategy: DFS dives deep, while BFS expands wide, affecting their performance and suitability for specific problems.

14. What is the difference between NP, NP-complete, and NP-hard problems?
Answer: NP (nondeterministic polynomial time) problems are those for which a solution can be verified in polynomial

time. NP-complete problems are the hardest problems in NP, meaning any NP problem can be reduced to them in polynomial time. NP-hard problems are at least as hard as NP-complete problems but are not necessarily in NP (they may not have a verifiable solution in polynomial time). If a polynomial-time algorithm is found for any NP-complete problem, all NP problems become solvable in polynomial time, potentially proving P = NP — one of the most important open problems in computer science.

15. What is the Floyd-Warshall algorithm, and what is its time complexity?
Answer: The Floyd-Warshall algorithm is a dynamic programming algorithm used to find the shortest paths between all pairs of vertices in a weighted graph. It works for both directed and undirected graphs, including those with negative edge weights (but no negative cycles). The algorithm iteratively updates the shortest path matrix by considering each vertex as an intermediate point. The time complexity is $O(n^3)$, where n is the number of vertices. Despite its cubic time complexity, it is efficient for dense graphs or graphs with a small number of vertices and is easy to implement.

16. What is the role of binary search in algorithm design?
Answer: Binary search is a classic divide-and-conquer algorithm used to find elements in a sorted array efficiently. By repeatedly dividing the search interval in half, it reduces the time complexity to O(log n), making it significantly faster than linear search for large datasets. It is foundational in algorithm design, often used as a building block in more complex problems, such as finding boundaries, minimum/maximum values, or solving numerical approximations. Binary search also appears in applications like dictionaries, databases, and low-level systems programming where speed and accuracy are critical.

17. What is a spanning tree, and what are its applications?
Answer: A spanning tree is a subgraph of a connected, undirected graph that connects all the vertices without forming any cycles and with the minimum possible number of edges (n-1 edges for n vertices). Minimum spanning trees (MSTs) are widely used in network design, such as minimizing the cost of wiring connections between computers or cities. Algorithms like Kruskal's and Prim's help in efficiently constructing MSTs. Other applications include clustering, approximation algorithms, and creating efficient broadcast or multicast networks where redundancy must be minimized.

18. What is topological sorting, and where is it used?
Answer: Topological sorting is the linear ordering of vertices in a directed acyclic graph (DAG) such that for every directed edge $u \rightarrow v$, vertex u comes before v in the ordering. It is widely used in scheduling tasks, resolving symbol dependencies in linkers, and organizing data hierarchically. Topological sort is performed using either depth-first search (DFS) or Kahn's algorithm (using indegrees and a queue). It is only applicable to DAGs and is crucial in scenarios where tasks must be executed in a specific sequence without violating constraints.

19. What is the difference between divide-and-conquer and greedy techniques?
Answer: Divide-and-conquer algorithms break a problem into smaller subproblems, solve each recursively, and combine the results. This strategy is powerful for problems with overlapping substructure or where combining sub-solutions is straightforward. Greedy algorithms, however, make the best local choice at each step without revisiting previous decisions, aiming for a global optimum. While greedy algorithms are faster and simpler, they don't always guarantee an optimal solution. Examples include mergesort (divide-and-conquer) and Dijkstra's algorithm (greedy). The choice between them depends on the problem's structure and whether a greedy choice always leads to the best global solution.

20. What are the limitations of greedy algorithms?
Answer: Greedy algorithms are limited in their applicability because they make local optimum choices without considering the broader context. This can lead to suboptimal solutions for problems that do not exhibit the greedy-choice property and optimal substructure. For instance, the greedy approach fails for the 0/1 knapsack problem but works for its fractional variant. Another limitation is the lack of backtracking — once a decision is made, it cannot be changed. As a result, greedy algorithms require a thorough proof of correctness to ensure they produce the optimal result, which may not always be possible.

21. What is the KMP algorithm, and why is it efficient for pattern matching?
Answer: The Knuth-Morris-Pratt (KMP) algorithm is an efficient string-matching technique that avoids unnecessary comparisons by preprocessing the pattern into a prefix table (also known as the longest prefix suffix array). This table

enables the algorithm to shift the pattern by the correct amount when a mismatch occurs, rather than starting from the beginning. Its time complexity is O(n + m), where n is the length of the text and m is the length of the pattern. KMP is particularly efficient for applications like text editors, search engines, and bioinformatics, where fast and repeated pattern searches are necessary.

22. How does Kruskal's algorithm work for finding a minimum spanning tree?
Answer: Kruskal's algorithm is a greedy algorithm used to find the minimum spanning tree (MST) of a connected, undirected graph. It works by sorting all the edges of the graph in non-decreasing order of their weights and adding them one by one to the MST, as long as they don't form a cycle. A disjoint-set (union-find) data structure is used to detect cycles efficiently. The algorithm continues until the MST includes (V – 1) edges. Kruskal's algorithm is effective for sparse graphs and guarantees the MST with a time complexity of O(E log E), where E is the number of edges.

23. What is a hash function, and how is it used in algorithms?
Answer: A hash function is a function that converts input data of arbitrary size into a fixed-size hash value, often used for indexing and quick data retrieval. In algorithms, hash functions are crucial for implementing hash tables, which allow average-case constant time complexity for search, insert, and delete operations. They are widely used in databases, compiler symbol tables, cryptography, and caching. A good hash function minimizes collisions (different inputs producing the same hash) and distributes keys uniformly. Algorithms based on hashing provide significant speedups in applications requiring frequent lookup and comparison.

24. What is the Rabin-Karp algorithm and how does it use hashing?
Answer: The Rabin-Karp algorithm is a string matching algorithm that uses hashing to find any occurrence of a pattern in a text. It computes a hash value for the pattern and for each substring of the text of the same length. When a hash match is found, it compares the actual strings to confirm the match. The rolling hash technique is used to efficiently update hash values as the window moves through the text. The average-case time complexity is O(n + m), though the worst-case can be O(nm) due to hash collisions. It's effective for detecting plagiarism and searching multiple patterns.

25. What is the concept of amortized analysis in algorithms?
Answer: Amortized analysis is a method used to determine the average time complexity of an operation over a sequence of operations, rather than just the worst-case for a single operation. It provides a more accurate picture of performance in practical scenarios. For example, while resizing a dynamic array has a worst-case time of O(n), amortized over many insertions, the time per operation is O(1). There are three techniques for amortized analysis: aggregate method, accounting method, and potential method. It is commonly used in analyzing data structures like stacks, queues, hash tables, and dynamic arrays.

26. What are strongly connected components in a directed graph?
Answer: In a directed graph, a strongly connected component (SCC) is a maximal set of vertices such that there is a path from any vertex to every other vertex in the same component. SCCs are used to analyze graph structures, detect cycles, and identify modular subgraphs in large systems. Algorithms like Kosaraju's and Tarjan's are efficient methods for finding SCCs. These components are especially useful in applications like web crawling, dependency resolution, and software modularity analysis. Identifying SCCs helps simplify the structure of a graph by collapsing components into single nodes.

27. How does Dijkstra's algorithm handle weighted graphs?
Answer: Dijkstra's algorithm finds the shortest path from a single source vertex to all other vertices in a weighted, non-negative edge graph. It uses a priority queue (typically a min-heap) to repeatedly select the vertex with the minimum distance, then updates the distances of its neighbors if a shorter path is found. The algorithm ensures that each vertex is processed only once. Its time complexity is O(V log V + E) when implemented with a Fibonacci heap. Dijkstra's algorithm is widely used in network routing, GPS navigation systems, and real-time traffic management.

28. What is a DAG and its importance in algorithm design?
Answer: A Directed Acyclic Graph (DAG) is a directed graph with no cycles. DAGs are important in algorithm design because they represent dependencies and execution flows where cycles are not allowed, such as scheduling, data processing pipelines, and version control. Topological sorting can only be applied to DAGs. They ensure deterministic behavior in processes, making them ideal for compiler design (e.g., instruction scheduling), database query

optimization, and project planning (e.g., PERT/CPM charts). Algorithms on DAGs are efficient and often linear in complexity due to the absence of cycles.

29. What is a dynamic programming approach for solving the matrix chain multiplication problem?
Answer: The matrix chain multiplication problem seeks the most efficient way to multiply a given sequence of matrices. The order of multiplication affects the number of scalar multiplications. Dynamic programming solves this by computing the cost of multiplying each subsequence of matrices and storing the results in a table to avoid redundant calculations. The optimal solution is obtained by evaluating all possible parenthesizations using a bottom-up approach. The time complexity is $O(n^3)$, where n is the number of matrices. This technique is used in compiler optimizations and scientific computing for minimizing computation time.

30. What is an articulation point in a graph and its significance?
Answer: An articulation point (or cut vertex) in a graph is a vertex that, when removed along with its incident edges, increases the number of connected components of the graph. Identifying articulation points is crucial in network reliability analysis, where such vertices represent points of vulnerability. In depth-first search (DFS), articulation points can be identified using discovery time and low values. They are used in designing robust communication and transportation networks, where the goal is to minimize the impact of node failures by identifying and reinforcing critical connection points.

31. How does the Floyd-Warshall algorithm compute all pairs shortest paths?
Answer: The Floyd-Warshall algorithm is a dynamic programming method used to find the shortest paths between all pairs of vertices in a weighted graph. It works by progressively updating a distance matrix, where the entry at position (i, j) represents the shortest path from vertex i to vertex j. Initially, this matrix is filled with direct edge weights (or infinity if no direct edge exists). For each intermediate vertex k, the algorithm checks whether a path from i to j through k is shorter than the currently known path. Its time complexity is $O(n^3)$, making it suitable for dense graphs or when all-pairs shortest paths are needed, such as in network routing or path analysis.

32. What is the difference between BFS and DFS in terms of space and application?
Answer: Breadth-First Search (BFS) and Depth-First Search (DFS) are fundamental graph traversal algorithms with different behavior. BFS explores neighbors level by level using a queue, while DFS dives deep into each branch before backtracking, using a stack (either explicit or via recursion). BFS typically requires more memory, especially for wide graphs, since it stores all neighbors at the current depth. DFS, in contrast, is more space-efficient on wide graphs but can consume more memory on deep graphs. BFS is preferred for shortest path problems in unweighted graphs, while DFS is effective for topological sorting, cycle detection, and maze-solving.

33. What is the difference between greedy and dynamic programming approaches?
Answer: Greedy algorithms make locally optimal choices at each step with the hope of finding a global optimum, whereas dynamic programming (DP) solves problems by combining solutions to subproblems and storing results to avoid recomputation. Greedy algorithms are generally faster and easier to implement but don't always produce the optimal solution unless the problem has the **greedy-choice property** and **optimal substructure**. DP, though more computationally intensive, guarantees an optimal solution for problems with overlapping subproblems and optimal substructure. Examples include Dijkstra's (greedy) vs. Bellman-Ford (DP) for shortest paths, or fractional knapsack (greedy) vs. 0/1 knapsack (DP).

34. How does topological sorting work and when is it used?
Answer: Topological sorting is an ordering of vertices in a directed acyclic graph (DAG) such that for every directed edge $u \rightarrow v$, vertex u comes before v in the ordering. It is computed using either depth-first search (DFS) with a post-order stack or by Kahn's algorithm using indegree counting. Topological sorting is used in scenarios that involve task scheduling, build dependency resolution, and compilation order. It only applies to DAGs, and its time complexity is $O(V + E)$. The sort ensures that dependencies are respected, which is critical in many real-world systems like pipelines and job scheduling.

35. What is memoization and how is it different from tabulation?
Answer: Memoization is a top-down dynamic programming technique where recursive function calls are used and results of subproblems are stored (cached) to avoid redundant calculations. Tabulation, on the other hand, is a bottom-up approach that builds the solution iteratively using a table. Memoization is easier to implement using recursion but

may have more overhead due to the function call stack, while tabulation is generally more space and time-efficient. Both techniques aim to solve overlapping subproblems and are used in solving problems like Fibonacci number calculation, knapsack, and longest common subsequence.

36. What are approximation algorithms and why are they used?
Answer: Approximation algorithms are used for NP-hard problems where finding an exact optimal solution is computationally infeasible in polynomial time. These algorithms provide near-optimal solutions within a provable bound of the optimal result. They are used in problems like the Traveling Salesman Problem (TSP), vertex cover, and set cover. The quality of an approximation algorithm is measured by its approximation ratio, which compares the algorithm's solution cost to the optimal cost. These algorithms are critical in operations research, logistics, and scheduling where practical solutions are needed quickly.

37. Explain Prim's algorithm for minimum spanning tree.
Answer: Prim's algorithm is a greedy approach for finding a minimum spanning tree (MST) in a weighted, undirected graph. It starts from an arbitrary node and grows the MST by adding the smallest weight edge that connects a vertex in the tree to a vertex outside the tree. A priority queue or min-heap is typically used to select the next minimum edge efficiently. The algorithm ensures no cycles are formed. Its time complexity is O(E log V) using a binary heap. Prim's is effective for dense graphs and is widely used in network design and clustering.

38. What is a red-black tree and its properties?
Answer: A red-black tree is a self-balancing binary search tree where each node has an extra bit for color (red or black). It maintains balance through five key properties, including the root being black, red nodes not having red children, and all paths from a node to descendant leaves containing the same number of black nodes. These rules ensure the tree's height remains logarithmic, providing O(log n) time for insertion, deletion, and search. Red-black trees are used in many system libraries (e.g., C++ STL map/set) due to their guaranteed balance and efficiency.

39. How do divide and conquer algorithms work?
Answer: Divide and conquer is a strategy where a problem is divided into smaller subproblems, each solved independently and then combined to form the solution to the original problem. This approach works well when subproblems are similar and independent. Examples include Merge Sort, Quick Sort, Binary Search, and Strassen's matrix multiplication. It often results in algorithms with logarithmic or polynomial time complexities. Divide and conquer enhances performance by enabling parallelism and reducing time complexity through efficient recursive decomposition of tasks.

40. What is tail recursion and why is it important in algorithm design?
Answer: Tail recursion is a special kind of recursion where the recursive call is the last operation in the function. This allows some compilers and interpreters to optimize the recursion using tail-call optimization (TCO), which reuses the current function's stack frame instead of adding a new one. This prevents stack overflow and reduces space usage. Tail recursion is useful in functional programming and recursive algorithm design where deep recursion is expected. However, not all languages support TCO, so iterative alternatives are often preferred for performance-critical applications.

41. What is the amortized analysis of algorithms?
Answer: Amortized analysis is a technique used to determine the average time per operation over a sequence of operations, even if individual operations can be expensive in isolation. It gives a more realistic picture of an algorithm's performance in practical scenarios. There are three main methods for amortized analysis: aggregate method, accounting method, and potential method. This technique is commonly used in analyzing dynamic arrays, splay trees, and certain data structure operations like incrementing a binary counter or enqueue-dequeue in a queue with resizing. It ensures that occasional expensive operations are averaged out over time.

42. Explain the Rabin-Karp algorithm for pattern matching.
Answer: The Rabin-Karp algorithm is a string-searching algorithm that uses hashing to find any one of a set of pattern strings in a text. It calculates a hash value for the pattern and compares it with hash values of substrings of the text. If the hash matches, a character-by-character comparison is done to verify the match. It is efficient for multiple pattern matching, with average and best-case complexity of O(n + m), but can degrade to O(nm) in the worst case due to hash collisions. Rabin-Karp is particularly effective in plagiarism detection and spam filtering.

43. What are the characteristics of NP-complete problems?
Answer: NP-complete problems are a class of decision problems for which no known polynomial-time algorithm exists, but for which a proposed solution can be verified in polynomial time. These problems are both in NP and as hard as any problem in NP. If any NP-complete problem can be solved in polynomial time, then all NP problems can. Common NP-complete problems include the traveling salesman problem, knapsack problem, and boolean satisfiability (SAT). These problems are central to computational complexity theory and algorithmic research.

44. How does the Boyer-Moore algorithm improve pattern matching efficiency?
Answer: The Boyer-Moore algorithm improves pattern matching by scanning the pattern from right to left and using two heuristics: bad character and good suffix. When a mismatch occurs, it uses these rules to shift the pattern efficiently rather than moving one character at a time. This often allows it to skip large sections of the text, making it faster in practice than other algorithms like Knuth-Morris-Pratt (KMP). The worst-case time complexity is O(mn), but the average time is sublinear, which makes it efficient for large text files and practical applications.

45. What is a suffix tree and where is it used?
Answer: A suffix tree is a compressed trie of all the suffixes of a given string. It enables fast pattern matching, substring search, and various string operations in linear time. Constructing a suffix tree takes O(n) time and space using algorithms like Ukkonen's. Suffix trees are used in bioinformatics for genome analysis, in plagiarism detection, and in text editors for implementing features like autocomplete and find-and-replace. They also support efficient computation of longest repeated substrings and longest common substrings between two texts.

46. How is the Longest Common Subsequence (LCS) problem solved using dynamic programming?
Answer: The LCS problem is solved by building a 2D matrix where each cell (i, j) represents the length of the longest common subsequence of the first i characters of string A and the first j characters of string B. The recurrence relation is: if A[i] == B[j], then LCS[i][j] = 1 + LCS[i-1][j-1]; otherwise, LCS[i][j] = max(LCS[i-1][j], LCS[i][j-1]). The final answer is at LCS[m][n]. This algorithm runs in O(mn) time and is widely used in file comparison tools, diff utilities, and bioinformatics for DNA sequence alignment.

47. What is the difference between 0/1 knapsack and fractional knapsack problems?
Answer: In the 0/1 knapsack problem, items cannot be broken down; each item is either included or excluded from the knapsack. It is solved using dynamic programming with a time complexity of O(nW), where n is the number of items and W is the knapsack capacity. In contrast, the fractional knapsack problem allows breaking items into smaller parts and is solved using a greedy algorithm in O(n log n) time. While fractional knapsack always yields an optimal solution, 0/1 knapsack does not always follow a greedy approach and requires DP for accuracy.

48. What is the role of hashing in algorithm design?
Answer: Hashing is used in algorithm design to achieve constant-time average-case complexity for operations like search, insert, and delete. It involves mapping keys to hash values using a hash function and storing them in a hash table. Good hashing minimizes collisions, which are resolved using techniques like chaining or open addressing. Hashing is crucial in data structures like hash maps and sets, and is used in applications such as database indexing, cryptography, and caching. The choice of a good hash function and collision resolution strategy significantly affects performance.

49. Explain the Backtracking technique with an example.
Answer: Backtracking is an algorithmic technique for solving problems incrementally by trying partial solutions and then abandoning them if they do not lead to a viable solution. It is often used in constraint satisfaction problems like N-Queens, Sudoku, and permutations. For example, in the N-Queens problem, the algorithm places a queen in a column and recursively places queens in the next rows. If it finds a conflict, it backtracks and moves the queen. Though potentially exponential in time complexity, backtracking is practical for many small or moderate-sized input cases.

50. What are decision trees and their use in algorithm analysis?
Answer: Decision trees are tree-like models used for decision-making and classification. In algorithm analysis, they represent different possible outcomes based on input comparisons, particularly useful in analyzing comparison-based sorting algorithms. Each internal node represents a comparison, and each leaf node represents a sorted order of elements. The minimum height of a decision tree determines the lower bound of comparison-based sorting, which is

O(n log n). Decision trees are also used in machine learning for classification tasks and are the foundation of ensemble methods like Random Forests.

51. What is the purpose of memoization in dynamic programming?

Answer: Memoization is a technique used in dynamic programming to store the results of expensive function calls and return the cached result when the same inputs occur again. It avoids redundant computations by remembering previously solved subproblems. Memoization is typically implemented using a hash table or array, depending on the problem's nature. This optimization drastically improves the performance of recursive solutions, reducing exponential time complexity to polynomial in many cases. It is widely used in problems like Fibonacci number calculation, longest common subsequence, and matrix chain multiplication.

52. How does the Johnson's algorithm solve the all-pairs shortest path problem?

Answer: Johnson's algorithm finds the shortest paths between all pairs of vertices in a weighted, directed graph. It works even when some edge weights are negative, provided there are no negative-weight cycles. The algorithm first adds a new node connected to every other node with a zero-weight edge, then uses the Bellman-Ford algorithm to find shortest distances from the new node. It reweights the edges to remove negatives and then uses Dijkstra's algorithm from each vertex. The overall time complexity is $O(V^2 \log V + VE)$, making it efficient for sparse graphs.

53. Explain the concept of randomized algorithms with an example.

Answer: Randomized algorithms use random numbers at least once during computation to make decisions. These algorithms can have different outcomes on different runs, even with the same input. There are two types: Las Vegas (always correct, runtime varies) and Monte Carlo (fixed runtime, may give incorrect answers). An example is the Randomized QuickSort, which selects a pivot randomly, reducing the chance of worst-case time complexity. Randomized algorithms are also used in primality testing, load balancing, and cryptographic applications due to their simplicity and improved average performance.

54. What is the Clique problem in graph theory and its complexity?

Answer: The Clique problem involves determining whether a graph contains a complete subgraph (clique) of a specified size k. A clique is a subset of vertices where every pair is connected by an edge. The decision version of the problem is to check whether such a k-sized clique exists in the graph. The problem is NP-complete, meaning there is no known polynomial-time algorithm to solve it for all cases. Clique detection has applications in social network analysis, bioinformatics, and clustering but is computationally intensive due to its exponential complexity.

55. What are approximation algorithms and when are they used?

Answer: Approximation algorithms are used to find near-optimal solutions for NP-hard optimization problems where exact solutions are computationally infeasible. These algorithms guarantee a solution within a specific ratio of the optimal answer. They are particularly useful for problems like vertex cover, traveling salesman, and set cover. The performance of an approximation algorithm is measured by its approximation ratio. For example, a 2-approximation algorithm for the vertex cover problem guarantees a cover no more than twice the size of the optimal solution. They balance accuracy and efficiency.

56. How does the Edmonds-Karp algorithm improve Ford-Fulkerson for maximum flow?

Answer: The Edmonds-Karp algorithm is an implementation of the Ford-Fulkerson method using BFS to find augmenting paths in a flow network. It ensures that the shortest (in terms of edge count) augmenting path is used at each step, which improves performance over arbitrary DFS-based Ford-Fulkerson. This results in a time complexity of $O(VE^2)$, where V is the number of vertices and E is the number of edges. It avoids the pitfalls of infinite loops in irrational capacities and ensures convergence, making it more predictable and practical.

57. What is the concept of cut-vertices and bridges in a graph?

Answer: A cut-vertex (articulation point) is a vertex that, if removed, increases the number of connected components in a graph. A bridge (cut-edge) is an edge whose removal disconnects the graph. These are critical for network reliability analysis. Finding such elements is important in designing resilient communication and transportation networks. They can be identified using DFS traversal and tracking discovery and low times of each node. The presence of cut-vertices and bridges indicates vulnerabilities in the network that could be targeted or strengthened.

58. Explain the Karger's algorithm for finding the minimum cut in a graph.
Answer: Karger's algorithm is a randomized algorithm to compute the minimum cut of an undirected graph. It works by repeatedly selecting a random edge and contracting it, merging its endpoints, until only two vertices remain. The edges between these two vertices represent a cut. Due to its randomness, it may not always yield the minimum cut in one run, but repeating the algorithm multiple times increases the probability of finding the correct result. Its time complexity is $O(n^2 \log n)$, and it is appreciated for its simplicity and practical performance.

59. What are AVL trees and how do they maintain balance?
Answer: AVL trees are self-balancing binary search trees in which the difference between the heights of left and right subtrees (balance factor) is at most one for every node. After each insertion or deletion, the tree checks the balance factor and performs rotations (left, right, left-right, or right-left) to restore balance. This ensures O(log n) time complexity for insertion, deletion, and search operations. AVL trees are used where faster lookups and ordered data access are needed, such as in memory-intensive applications and database indexing.

60. What is the application of Bellman-Ford algorithm in networking?
Answer: The Bellman-Ford algorithm is used to compute shortest paths from a single source vertex to all other vertices in a graph, accommodating graphs with negative weight edges. In networking, it is used in distance-vector routing protocols like RIP (Routing Information Protocol), where routers share information with neighbors to determine the shortest path to destinations. Bellman-Ford is preferred in distributed environments because of its simplicity and ability to handle dynamic updates. However, its time complexity of O(VE) makes it less efficient than Dijkstra's for non-negative weights.

61. What are strongly connected components in a directed graph?
Answer: In a directed graph, a strongly connected component (SCC) is a maximal subset of vertices such that every vertex is reachable from every other vertex in the subset. In other words, for any two vertices u and v in the SCC, there exists a path from u to v and from v to u. SCCs help decompose complex graphs into simpler parts for analysis and are useful in various applications like compiler optimization, circuit design, and social network analysis. Algorithms like Kosaraju's and Tarjan's are used to find SCCs efficiently.

62. What is the purpose of a recurrence relation in algorithm analysis?
Answer: A recurrence relation expresses the overall time complexity of a recursive algorithm in terms of its smaller subproblems. It defines a function in terms of its value on smaller inputs and is used to analyze the running time of divide-and-conquer algorithms like merge sort and quicksort. For example, merge sort's recurrence is $T(n) = 2T(n/2) + O(n)$. Solving the recurrence using methods like substitution, recursion trees, or the Master Theorem provides the algorithm's time complexity, helping to evaluate its efficiency.

63. What is a disjoint-set data structure and where is it used?
Answer: A disjoint-set data structure, also known as Union-Find, keeps track of a set of elements partitioned into disjoint (non-overlapping) subsets. It supports two primary operations: **Find** (determines which subset a particular element belongs to) and **Union** (merges two subsets into one). It is mainly used in network connectivity, Kruskal's algorithm for finding minimum spanning trees, and in algorithms that manage equivalence relations. Efficient implementations use techniques like path compression and union by rank to ensure nearly constant time operations.

64. What is the greedy method and its main strategy?
Answer: The greedy method is an algorithmic paradigm that builds up a solution piece by piece, always choosing the option that offers the most immediate benefit or looks best at that moment. It does not consider future consequences but hopes that a local optimum choice leads to a global optimum. This strategy works well for problems that exhibit greedy-choice property and optimal substructure, such as the fractional knapsack, Huffman coding, and activity selection problems. When these conditions aren't met, greedy algorithms may fail to find the optimal solution.

65. Describe the concept of a minimum spanning forest.
Answer: A minimum spanning forest (MSF) is a union of minimum spanning trees (MSTs) for each connected component of a disconnected, undirected, weighted graph. Since MSTs only apply to connected graphs, when the graph is not fully connected, we find an MST for each component, collectively called the MSF. Algorithms like Kruskal's can be applied directly to compute the MSF, treating each component separately. MSFs are useful in

network design when the overall network might not be fully interconnected but still requires optimal sub-network construction.

66. What is the longest common subsequence problem and its application?

Answer: The Longest Common Subsequence (LCS) problem involves finding the longest sequence of characters that appear left-to-right (not necessarily consecutively) in both given strings. It is a classic dynamic programming problem with applications in diff utilities, version control systems (like Git), bioinformatics for DNA sequence analysis, and plagiarism detection. The standard approach builds a DP table with time complexity O(mn), where m and n are lengths of the two strings. It helps identify similarities between texts and sequences efficiently.

67. How does the Rabin-Karp algorithm improve string matching?

Answer: The Rabin-Karp algorithm enhances string matching by using hashing to compare the pattern with substrings of the text. It computes a hash value for the pattern and compares it with hash values of substrings of the same length in the text. If a hash match occurs, it performs a character-by-character comparison to confirm. This reduces the average-case complexity to O(n + m), where n is the text length and m is the pattern length. It is efficient when searching for multiple patterns simultaneously.

68. What are graph traversal techniques and their applications?

Answer: The two main graph traversal techniques are Breadth-First Search (BFS) and Depth-First Search (DFS). BFS explores neighbors level by level and is used for shortest path in unweighted graphs, network broadcasting, and finding connected components. DFS explores as far as possible along each branch before backtracking, useful in topological sorting, cycle detection, and solving mazes. Both algorithms are fundamental in analyzing graph structures, and their implementations serve as building blocks for many advanced algorithms in computer science.

69. What is the Hamiltonian Path problem and its complexity?

Answer: The Hamiltonian Path problem asks whether a path exists in a graph that visits each vertex exactly once. If such a path starts and ends at the same vertex, it's called a Hamiltonian Cycle. This problem is NP-complete, making it computationally intractable for large graphs using brute-force methods. It has applications in routing, scheduling, and puzzle solving. Due to its complexity, approximation, heuristic, or backtracking techniques are often used to handle practical instances.

70. What is the difference between NP, NP-complete, and NP-hard problems?

Answer: NP (nondeterministic polynomial time) is a class of problems for which solutions can be verified in polynomial time. NP-complete problems are the hardest problems in NP; if one NP-complete problem has a polynomial-time solution, all NP problems do. NP-hard problems are at least as hard as NP-complete problems but do not have to be in NP, meaning their solutions may not be verifiable in polynomial time. Examples include SAT (NP-complete) and the Halting Problem (NP-hard but not in NP).

71. What is the Bellman-Ford algorithm and how does it differ from Dijkstra's algorithm?

Answer: The Bellman-Ford algorithm finds the shortest path from a single source to all other vertices in a weighted graph and supports negative weights, unlike Dijkstra's algorithm. It works by relaxing all edges $|V| - 1$ times, where V is the number of vertices. Bellman-Ford can detect negative weight cycles, which Dijkstra's algorithm cannot. However, Bellman-Ford has higher time complexity, O(VE), compared to Dijkstra's O((V + E) log V) using a min-priority queue. This makes Bellman-Ford preferable in scenarios with potential negative weights, while Dijkstra's is more efficient for non-negative weighted graphs.

72. What is the role of dynamic programming in algorithm design?

Answer: Dynamic programming (DP) is a technique used to solve problems by breaking them down into overlapping subproblems, solving each subproblem only once, and storing the result. This avoids redundant computations and improves efficiency, especially for optimization problems. DP is applied to problems like the Fibonacci sequence, matrix chain multiplication, knapsack problem, and shortest path problems. It is particularly useful when a problem exhibits both optimal substructure and overlapping subproblems. By using memoization or tabulation, DP offers a significant speed-up over naïve recursive approaches.

73. What is the difference between a greedy algorithm and dynamic programming?

Answer: Greedy algorithms make the locally optimal choice at each step with the hope of finding a global optimum, while dynamic programming considers all possible solutions and stores the best one by solving subproblems. Greedy algorithms are typically faster and easier to implement but may not always provide the optimal solution. Dynamic programming ensures an optimal solution but may require more computation and memory. A classic example where greedy fails and DP succeeds is the 0/1 knapsack problem. Each method is suitable for specific problem types depending on their structure.

74. What is the purpose of backtracking in algorithms?
Answer: Backtracking is a recursive technique used for solving problems incrementally, by building a solution piece by piece and removing solutions that fail to meet constraints. It is often used in decision problems such as puzzles, pathfinding, and combinatorial optimization (e.g., Sudoku, N-Queens, subset sum). Backtracking involves exploring possible options and abandoning them ("backtrack") when it becomes clear that they cannot lead to a valid solution. It is a depth-first search strategy and is effective when the solution space is large but can be pruned significantly.

75. What are the applications of the Floyd-Warshall algorithm?
Answer: The Floyd-Warshall algorithm is used to find the shortest paths between all pairs of vertices in a weighted graph. It is especially useful in dense graphs and graphs with both positive and negative edge weights (excluding negative cycles). Applications include network routing, urban traffic navigation, and map-based services that require precomputation of all shortest paths. It uses dynamic programming and has a time complexity of $O(V^3)$. Floyd-Warshall is also helpful in transitive closure problems and can be modified to reconstruct paths.

76. What is amortized analysis in algorithm design?
Answer: Amortized analysis is used to determine the average time complexity of an operation over a sequence of operations, ensuring that the average cost remains low even if some operations are expensive. Unlike worst-case analysis, it considers the total cost across multiple operations. Common techniques include aggregate, accounting, and potential methods. A classic example is the dynamic array resizing, where most insertions are O(1), but occasional resizing is O(n); amortized analysis shows that the average time per insertion is still O(1). It provides more realistic performance estimates in practice.

77. What is a spanning tree, and how is it useful in computer networks?
Answer: A spanning tree of a graph is a subgraph that includes all the vertices of the original graph, is connected, and contains no cycles. In computer networks, spanning trees are crucial for designing efficient and loop-free network topologies, such as in Ethernet switching using the Spanning Tree Protocol (STP). Spanning trees minimize the number of connections while maintaining network reachability. Algorithms like Kruskal's and Prim's are used to construct minimum spanning trees (MST), which optimize the total edge weight, helping reduce cost and complexity in network design.

78. What is the divide and conquer strategy in algorithm design?
Answer: Divide and conquer is an algorithm design paradigm that works by dividing a problem into smaller subproblems, solving each recursively, and combining their solutions. It is effective for problems where subproblems are independent and of the same type. Classic examples include merge sort, quicksort, binary search, and Strassen's matrix multiplication. Divide and conquer improves efficiency by reducing problem size and applying recursion. It often leads to logarithmic or linearithmic time complexities, making it a powerful tool in computational problem solving.

79. What is the difference between recursive and iterative algorithms?
Answer: Recursive algorithms solve a problem by calling themselves with smaller inputs until reaching a base case. Iterative algorithms use loops to repeat operations until a condition is met. Recursion is often more intuitive and used in problems like tree traversal, while iteration is typically more efficient in terms of memory and sometimes speed. Recursion incurs function call overhead and risks stack overflow, whereas iteration uses constant space. The choice between recursion and iteration depends on the problem's structure and constraints.

80. What is the use of the topological sort algorithm?
Answer: Topological sorting is used to order the vertices of a Directed Acyclic Graph (DAG) such that for every directed edge u → v, vertex u comes before v in the ordering. It is widely used in scheduling tasks, resolving symbol dependencies in compilers, determining build order in software projects, and data serialization. Topological sort is

only applicable to DAGs and can be implemented using depth-first search or Kahn's algorithm. It ensures a valid execution sequence respecting all dependencies, making it essential in dependency resolution systems.

81. What is the Master Theorem in algorithm analysis?

Answer: The Master Theorem provides a way to determine the time complexity of divide-and-conquer algorithms. It is used for recurrence relations of the form $T(n) = aT(n/b) + f(n)$, where $a \geq 1$, $b > 1$, and $f(n)$ is an asymptotically positive function. Based on the comparison of f(n) with n^log_b(a), the theorem categorizes the solution into three cases to find the time complexity. It simplifies the analysis of algorithms like merge sort, binary search, and Strassen's matrix multiplication without needing to expand the recurrence repeatedly.

82. What is memoization and how does it improve performance?

Answer: Memoization is a technique used in dynamic programming where the results of expensive function calls are stored and reused when the same inputs occur again. It avoids redundant calculations and is particularly effective in recursive algorithms with overlapping subproblems, such as Fibonacci computation or shortest path problems. Memoization can be implemented using arrays, hash tables, or dictionaries. It converts exponential-time recursive algorithms into polynomial-time solutions by eliminating repeated work, significantly improving performance in large-scale computations.

83. What is the Travelling Salesman Problem (TSP) and why is it hard?

Answer: The Travelling Salesman Problem (TSP) asks for the shortest possible route that visits each city exactly once and returns to the origin city. It is an NP-hard problem, meaning that no known polynomial-time algorithm can solve it for all cases. The difficulty arises from the factorial number of permutations to evaluate (n!), making brute-force infeasible for large inputs. Approximation algorithms and heuristics like genetic algorithms, nearest neighbor, and dynamic programming (for small n) are used to tackle TSP in real-world scenarios such as logistics and route optimization.

84. What is meant by algorithmic complexity?

Answer: Algorithmic complexity refers to the resources required by an algorithm to solve a problem, typically measured in terms of time (time complexity) and space (space complexity). It provides a theoretical estimation of the algorithm's efficiency based on input size. Time complexity expresses how the computation time grows with input, while space complexity measures memory usage. Big-O notation is commonly used to express upper bounds. Understanding complexity helps in selecting or designing efficient algorithms suited for particular applications and constraints.

85. What is the difference between time complexity and space complexity?

Answer: Time complexity refers to the amount of time an algorithm takes to complete as a function of input size, while space complexity measures the amount of memory used during execution. An algorithm with low time complexity may have high space requirements, and vice versa. For example, merge sort has time complexity $O(n \log n)$ and space complexity $O(n)$, whereas quicksort has similar time complexity but lower space complexity. Optimizing both is crucial for developing efficient and scalable algorithms.

86. What is the N-Queens problem and how is it solved?

Answer: The N-Queens problem involves placing N chess queens on an $N \times N$ board so that no two queens threaten each other. It is typically solved using backtracking, where queens are placed row by row, and invalid positions are skipped using constraints. The algorithm backtracks whenever it encounters a conflict, eventually producing all valid configurations. It exemplifies constraint satisfaction problems and is widely used to teach recursion and backtracking in algorithm design due to its elegant logic and combinatorial nature.

87. What is meant by recursion depth and how does it affect algorithm performance?

Answer: Recursion depth refers to the number of active recursive calls on the call stack at a given time. A deep recursion can lead to stack overflow if the system's maximum stack size is exceeded. It also affects performance since each call consumes memory and may add function call overhead. Tail-recursive functions or converting recursion to iteration can help manage or reduce recursion depth. Optimizing recursion depth is important in algorithms like DFS, quicksort, or Fibonacci calculations.

88. What are the characteristics of NP-complete problems?
Answer: NP-complete problems are a class of problems in NP (nondeterministic polynomial time) that are both NP-hard and verifiable in polynomial time. They are significant because if one NP-complete problem can be solved in polynomial time, all NP problems can. Characteristics include being verifiable quickly, having no known polynomial-time solution, and the ability to be reduced from one NP-complete problem to another. Examples include the satisfiability problem (SAT), TSP, and knapsack. These problems are central to computational theory and complexity.

89. How does Kruskal's algorithm work and when is it preferred?
Answer: Kruskal's algorithm finds a minimum spanning tree by sorting all edges in non-decreasing order and adding them one by one to the MST if they don't form a cycle. A disjoint-set data structure is used to efficiently detect cycles. It is preferred in sparse graphs with fewer edges compared to the number of vertices, as its time complexity is O(E log E). Kruskal's algorithm is simple and effective for graphs where edge sorting is not a performance bottleneck.

90. What is the use of hashing in algorithm design?
Answer: Hashing is a technique used to map data to a fixed-size table using a hash function. It allows for constant-time average complexity in operations like insert, delete, and search. Hashing is widely used in data structures such as hash tables, symbol tables, and caches. Good hash functions minimize collisions and distribute entries uniformly. Hashing is crucial in algorithms dealing with large datasets, such as duplicate detection, indexing, and associative arrays, improving overall algorithm efficiency.

91. What are approximation algorithms and when are they used?
Answer: Approximation algorithms are used for NP-hard problems where exact solutions are computationally infeasible. They provide near-optimal solutions with a guaranteed performance bound. These algorithms are used in real-world applications like scheduling, network design, and TSP. For example, the greedy algorithm for vertex cover guarantees a solution no worse than twice the optimal. Approximation algorithms trade accuracy for efficiency and are valuable when acceptable solutions are sufficient, and time constraints are critical.

92. What is the Rabin-Karp algorithm used for?
Answer: The Rabin-Karp algorithm is a string-searching algorithm that uses hashing to find any one of a set of pattern strings in a text. It computes a hash value for the pattern and then compares it with the hash values of substrings in the text. If a match is found, it performs a direct comparison to confirm. The average-case complexity is O(n + m), but worst-case is O(nm). Rabin-Karp is efficient for multiple pattern searches and plagiarism detection.

93. What is the significance of graph traversal algorithms?
Answer: Graph traversal algorithms like Breadth-First Search (BFS) and Depth-First Search (DFS) are essential for exploring nodes and edges in graphs. They are used in applications such as finding connected components, shortest paths, topological sorting, and detecting cycles. BFS is ideal for finding the shortest path in unweighted graphs, while DFS is used for backtracking and path enumeration. Graph traversal forms the basis for many complex graph algorithms and is crucial in computer science and AI.

94. What is the Longest Common Subsequence (LCS) problem?
Answer: The Longest Common Subsequence (LCS) problem involves finding the longest sequence that appears in the same order (not necessarily contiguous) in two strings. It is solved using dynamic programming in O(mn) time, where m and n are the lengths of the strings. LCS is used in diff tools, DNA sequence analysis, and file comparison. It demonstrates optimal substructure and overlapping subproblems, making it a textbook application of dynamic programming.

95. What are greedy-choice properties in algorithms?
Answer: The greedy-choice property implies that a locally optimal choice leads to a globally optimal solution. For an algorithm to work greedily, it must satisfy this property and the optimal substructure property. Greedy algorithms do not reconsider choices and thus require the problem to be well-structured. Examples include activity selection, Huffman coding, and fractional knapsack. If a problem lacks the greedy-choice property, greedy algorithms may not yield correct or optimal solutions.

96. What is the role of priority queues in algorithm implementation?
Answer: Priority queues are abstract data types where each element has a priority, and elements with higher priority are served before others. They are typically implemented using heaps (binary, binomial, or Fibonacci). Priority queues are used in Dijkstra's algorithm, Prim's algorithm, job scheduling, and simulation systems. They help in efficiently retrieving and updating elements with the highest or lowest priority, making them integral in numerous greedy and graph algorithms.

97. How does Quickselect algorithm work?
Answer: Quickselect is a selection algorithm to find the k-th smallest element in an unordered list. It is related to quicksort and uses partitioning to narrow down the search space. At each step, it partitions the array and recursively searches only in the part that contains the k-th element. Its average-case time complexity is O(n), although the worst-case is $O(n^2)$. It is used in median finding and statistical data analysis when full sorting is unnecessary.

98. What is the importance of the cut property in MST algorithms?
Answer: The cut property states that, for any cut in a connected, weighted graph, the minimum-weight edge crossing the cut belongs to the minimum spanning tree (MST). This principle is fundamental in MST algorithms like Kruskal's and Prim's. It ensures that by selecting the lightest edge crossing any cut, one can incrementally build an MST without forming cycles. The cut property helps in proving the correctness of MST algorithms and optimizing edge selection.

99. What is the use of the Union-Find data structure?
Answer: The Union-Find (disjoint-set) data structure efficiently handles dynamic connectivity problems. It supports two main operations: find, to determine which set a particular element belongs to, and union, to merge two sets. It is widely used in Kruskal's algorithm for cycle detection and network connectivity. With optimizations like path compression and union by rank, it achieves nearly constant time per operation, making it highly efficient for partitioning and clustering problems.

100. What are recurrence relations and how are they solved?
Answer: Recurrence relations define sequences where each term is a function of preceding terms. They commonly arise in analyzing recursive algorithms. Solving recurrence relations helps determine the time complexity of such algorithms. Methods to solve them include substitution, recursion tree, and Master Theorem. For example, T(n) = 2T(n/2) + n represents merge sort and solves to O(n log n). Understanding and solving recurrence relations is crucial for accurate algorithm analysis.

101. What is the difference between divide-and-conquer and dynamic programming?
Answer: Divide-and-conquer solves problems by breaking them into independent subproblems, solving each recursively, and combining results. Examples include quicksort and mergesort. In contrast, dynamic programming is used when subproblems overlap and recomputation is avoided by storing solutions. Problems like Fibonacci series, matrix chain multiplication, and knapsack are efficiently solved using dynamic programming. While divide-and-conquer uses recursion only, dynamic programming also includes memoization or tabulation to optimize performance.

102. What is amortized analysis and why is it important?
Answer: Amortized analysis evaluates the average time per operation over a sequence, guaranteeing performance even if some operations are costly. Unlike worst-case analysis, it provides a more realistic average case. It's particularly useful in data structures like dynamic arrays, splay trees, and union-find where occasional expensive operations are offset by many cheap ones. This analysis ensures predictable performance in aggregate and helps optimize algorithm design for consistent results.

103. Explain the concept of bit manipulation in algorithms.
Answer: Bit manipulation involves using bitwise operators (AND, OR, XOR, NOT, shifts) to perform fast, memory-efficient operations. It's used in tasks like checking if a number is even/odd, counting set bits, or swapping values without extra space. Bit manipulation is highly optimized at the hardware level, often replacing loops with single operations. Algorithms involving subsets, masks, or binary representations benefit significantly from these techniques, particularly in competitive programming and embedded systems.

104. How does binary search work and when should it be used?
Answer: Binary search efficiently finds an element in a sorted list by repeatedly dividing the search interval in half. It starts with the middle element and eliminates half of the list based on comparison. Its time complexity is O(log n), making it suitable for large sorted datasets. Binary search is widely used in searching problems, finding bounds, or conditions in monotonic functions. It's essential for optimizing algorithms and search-heavy applications.

105. What are space-efficient algorithms and why are they necessary?
Answer: Space-efficient algorithms are designed to minimize memory usage while maintaining acceptable time complexity. They are crucial in systems with limited resources or large data. Techniques include in-place operations, bitwise storage, and space-optimized dynamic programming (like using two rows instead of a full matrix). Applications like mobile computing, embedded systems, and large-scale data processing benefit from these algorithms, ensuring performance without exhausting memory.

106. What is the principle behind topological sorting?
Answer: Topological sorting orders vertices of a Directed Acyclic Graph (DAG) so that for every directed edge (u, v), vertex u comes before v. It's used in task scheduling, build systems, and resolving dependencies. Algorithms like Kahn's algorithm or DFS-based approaches are used to compute it. Topological sorting is only applicable to DAGs and forms the basis for detecting cycles or planning ordered execution in systems.

107. Explain the greedy algorithm used for coin change.
Answer: The greedy approach for coin change selects the largest denomination not exceeding the remaining amount, repeating until the total is formed. It works optimally only for certain coin systems like US denominations but fails for arbitrary sets (e.g., {1, 3, 4}). While fast (O(n) with sorting), it's not always optimal. Dynamic programming is often preferred to guarantee the minimum number of coins for any denomination set.

108. What is the Bellman-Ford algorithm and how does it compare to Dijkstra's?
Answer: Bellman-Ford finds the shortest path from a source to all vertices in a weighted graph, including those with negative weights. It relaxes all edges up to (V−1) times and detects negative weight cycles. Unlike Dijkstra's, it works for graphs with negative weights but is slower with O(VE) time. Dijkstra's is more efficient (O(V log V + E)) but fails with negative weights. Bellman-Ford is used in routing and error checking.

109. What is the significance of tail recursion in algorithms?
Answer: Tail recursion is a recursion where the recursive call is the last operation. It allows compilers to optimize by reusing stack frames, reducing memory usage. Tail-recursive functions can be transformed into iterative forms, improving performance. It's significant in functional programming and recursive algorithms like factorial or GCD, ensuring stack efficiency and preventing overflow.

110. How do you solve recurrence relations using recursion trees?
Answer: Recursion trees visualize the recursive calls and their costs to estimate total complexity. Each level represents subproblem calls, and their costs are summed level by level. For instance, in $T(n) = 2T(n/2) + n$, the tree shows log n levels with total cost O(n log n). This method provides an intuitive understanding of time complexity and helps identify dominant costs in recursive algorithms.

111. What is backtracking and how does it differ from recursion?
Answer: Backtracking is a systematic trial-and-error method for solving constraint problems by exploring all possible configurations. It uses recursion to try options and backtracks when constraints are violated. Unlike plain recursion, it incorporates decision-making and pruning. Problems like Sudoku, N-Queens, and subset generation use backtracking to reduce search space and find valid solutions efficiently.

112. How is graph coloring solved using backtracking?
Answer: Graph coloring assigns colors to vertices so that adjacent vertices have different colors. Backtracking tries each color and checks constraints recursively. If a valid assignment isn't possible, it backtracks to try another color. The algorithm explores all combinations, ensuring correctness. Though exponential in worst-case, it efficiently solves small or moderately sized graphs and is foundational in register allocation and scheduling.

113. What is a randomized algorithm? Give an example.
Answer: A randomized algorithm uses random numbers to influence behavior or decision-making. It may yield different outcomes for the same input but often achieves better average-case performance. Example: Randomized quicksort chooses pivot randomly to avoid worst-case performance. Monte Carlo algorithms may be incorrect with small probability, while Las Vegas algorithms always produce correct results with random runtimes.

114. What is a branching factor in algorithms?
Answer: Branching factor refers to the number of child nodes each node expands into during search or recursion. In tree-based problems, higher branching factors lead to exponential growth in computation. It's critical in evaluating the feasibility and complexity of search algorithms like DFS or BFS. Optimizing branching factor improves performance by pruning unneeded paths or using heuristics.

115. What is the difference between polynomial time and exponential time algorithms?
Answer: Polynomial-time algorithms have time complexity expressed as n^k (e.g., $O(n^2)$), making them scalable for large inputs. Exponential-time algorithms grow as k^n or faster, becoming infeasible quickly. Problems solvable in polynomial time are considered tractable, while those requiring exponential time (like TSP or SAT) are typically intractable. The distinction is fundamental in complexity theory and algorithm classification.

116. How does the concept of reducibility help in algorithm analysis?
Answer: Reducibility allows transforming one problem into another, preserving computational equivalence. If a known hard problem reduces to another, the latter is also hard. It helps classify problems (e.g., NP-complete) and prove their difficulty. For instance, reducing 3-SAT to CLIQUE shows CLIQUE is NP-complete. It guides algorithm design by leveraging solutions from similar problems.

117. What are flow networks and how are they solved?
Answer: Flow networks consist of directed graphs with capacities on edges, modeling systems like pipelines or traffic. The max-flow problem finds the greatest possible flow from source to sink, respecting capacities. Algorithms like Ford-Fulkerson and Edmonds-Karp solve it using augmenting paths and BFS/DFS. Applications include network routing, project scheduling, and image segmentation.

118. Explain the concept of cut vertices and bridges in graphs.
Answer: Cut vertices (articulation points) are nodes whose removal increases graph components. Bridges are edges that disconnect the graph when removed. They are identified using DFS and low-link values. These concepts help analyze graph reliability and are used in network design, fault tolerance, and biconnected component detection.

119. What is a sparse graph and how does it affect algorithm design?
Answer: A sparse graph has relatively few edges compared to vertices, typically O(V). It influences algorithm choice, where adjacency lists outperform matrices in space and performance. Algorithms like Kruskal's benefit from sparse graphs due to fewer edge evaluations. Understanding sparsity guides memory and runtime optimization.

120. What is the advantage of iterative deepening search (IDS)?
Answer: IDS combines depth-limited DFS and BFS advantages by progressively increasing depth limits. It ensures optimality like BFS but uses less memory like DFS. Each iteration performs a DFS up to a certain depth. Though nodes are revisited, the overhead is small compared to exponential growth. It's used in AI and puzzle solving (e.g., 8-puzzle).

121. What is the Chinese Remainder Theorem (CRT) in algorithms?
Answer: CRT provides a way to solve systems of congruences with pairwise coprime moduli. It reconstructs integers from their remainders modulo several pairwise coprime bases. CRT is vital in modular arithmetic, number theory, and cryptography (e.g., RSA optimization). Its algorithmic implementation requires computing modular inverses and applying them with given remainders.

122. How is parallelism applied in algorithm design?
Answer: Parallelism divides a problem into subproblems solved concurrently on multiple processors or threads. It reduces execution time, especially for large-scale data processing. Algorithms like parallel mergesort, matrix

multiplication, and graph traversal utilize parallelism. Challenges include synchronization, data dependencies, and load balancing. Parallel algorithms are essential in high-performance computing and multicore environments.

123. What is the difference between synchronous and asynchronous algorithms?
Answer: Synchronous algorithms proceed in lockstep, where all parts move together per cycle. Asynchronous algorithms allow independent progression without waiting for others. Synchronous models are easier to analyze but less flexible. Asynchronous systems are fault-tolerant and efficient under variable loads but harder to debug. Distributed systems, real-time systems, and networking often require asynchronous algorithms.

124. What is a heuristic algorithm and when is it useful?
Answer: Heuristics are problem-solving techniques that find good-enough solutions quickly when optimal ones are costly. They're useful in NP-hard problems like TSP, scheduling, and game playing. Heuristics use domain knowledge or approximations to guide search (e.g., A* algorithm). Though they lack guarantees, they provide practical performance for large or complex problems.

125. What is alpha-beta pruning in game tree algorithms?
Answer: Alpha-beta pruning optimizes minimax algorithms by eliminating branches that won't affect the outcome. Alpha represents the best value the maximizer can guarantee, while beta represents the minimizer's best. If a branch can't improve the outcome, it's pruned, reducing computation. It maintains optimality and is crucial in games like chess, reducing search depth significantly.

126. What is the significance of amortized analysis in algorithm design?
Answer: Amortized analysis is used to evaluate the average time per operation over a sequence of operations, ensuring more realistic performance expectations in the long run. Unlike worst-case analysis, which only considers the cost of the most expensive operation, amortized analysis distributes the cost across all operations. This technique is particularly useful in data structures like dynamic arrays, splay trees, and disjoint sets where occasional costly operations are balanced by many cheaper ones. Amortized analysis offers a more accurate and reliable picture of an algorithm's performance, aiding in better algorithm design and selection.

127. How does Kruskal's algorithm work for finding the minimum spanning tree?
Answer: Kruskal's algorithm finds a minimum spanning tree (MST) in a graph by sorting all edges in non-decreasing order of their weights and adding them one by one to the MST, ensuring no cycles are formed. It uses the Union-Find data structure to check for cycles efficiently. Initially, each vertex is in its own set. As edges are added, sets are merged if the edge connects two different sets. The process continues until the MST has (V-1) edges for a graph with V vertices. Kruskal's algorithm is efficient and suitable for sparse graphs.

128. What is the principle behind the greedy method in algorithm design?
Answer: The greedy method makes a sequence of choices, each of which is locally optimal, with the hope that this leads to a globally optimal solution. It builds the solution step-by-step, selecting the best option at each stage without reconsidering previous decisions. Greedy algorithms are simple and efficient, often used for optimization problems like activity selection, Huffman coding, and minimum spanning trees. However, they don't always yield optimal solutions, so it's crucial to ensure the problem satisfies the greedy-choice property and optimal substructure.

129. What is backtracking, and when is it used?
Answer: Backtracking is a general algorithmic technique for solving constraint satisfaction problems by incrementally building candidates for the solution and abandoning a candidate as soon as it is determined that it cannot lead to a valid solution. It is particularly effective for problems involving permutations, combinations, and partitioning, such as the N-Queens problem, Sudoku solving, and subset sum. Backtracking is a refined brute-force approach that uses recursion and pruning, making it more efficient than exhaustive search in many scenarios.

130. Explain the concept of branch and bound technique.
Answer: Branch and bound is an algorithm design paradigm for solving combinatorial optimization problems like the traveling salesman problem (TSP) and integer programming. It involves exploring the solution space in a tree-like fashion, branching into subproblems, and calculating a bound for each. If a subproblem's bound is worse than the best-known solution, it is discarded (pruned). This avoids unnecessary computation by eliminating unpromising

branches. The method guarantees finding an optimal solution, though its efficiency greatly depends on how tight the bounds and effective the pruning strategy are.

131. What is the role of dynamic programming in algorithm design?
Answer: Dynamic programming (DP) is a technique used to solve problems by breaking them down into overlapping subproblems and solving each subproblem only once, storing the results for future reference (memoization). It is especially useful when a problem exhibits optimal substructure, meaning the optimal solution can be constructed from optimal solutions of its subproblems. DP significantly reduces time complexity compared to naive recursive approaches. Classic examples include the Fibonacci sequence, shortest paths (e.g., Floyd-Warshall), and the knapsack problem. It is a powerful tool in algorithm design for optimization problems.

132. What is the difference between divide and conquer and dynamic programming?
Answer: Both divide and conquer and dynamic programming break problems into subproblems, but they differ in how they handle those subproblems. Divide and conquer divides problems into independent subproblems, solves them recursively, and combines their results. In contrast, dynamic programming deals with overlapping subproblems and stores their solutions to avoid redundant computations. While divide and conquer is used in algorithms like quicksort and mergesort, dynamic programming is applied to problems like the knapsack, matrix chain multiplication, and longest common subsequence. The choice between them depends on the problem's structure.

133. What is the purpose of the Floyd-Warshall algorithm?
Answer: The Floyd-Warshall algorithm is an all-pairs shortest path algorithm used to find the shortest paths between all pairs of vertices in a weighted graph. It uses dynamic programming to iteratively update the shortest distances by considering all intermediate vertices. The algorithm maintains a distance matrix, and for each pair of vertices (i, j), it checks whether including another vertex k in the path from i to j would result in a shorter path. It works for graphs with positive or negative edge weights but not with negative weight cycles.

134. What is a recurrence relation in the context of algorithms?
Answer: A recurrence relation is a mathematical expression that defines a sequence of values using recursion. In the context of algorithms, it is often used to represent the time complexity of recursive algorithms. For example, the recurrence for merge sort is $T(n) = 2T(n/2) + O(n)$, representing the division of the array into two halves and the merging step. Solving recurrence relations helps in analyzing the performance of recursive algorithms. Techniques like the Master Theorem, iteration method, and recursion tree are used to solve them.

135. What is the Master Theorem and how is it used?
Answer: The Master Theorem provides a direct way to determine the time complexity of divide-and-conquer algorithms of the form $T(n) = aT(n/b) + f(n)$, where $a \geq 1$, $b > 1$, and f(n) is an asymptotically positive function. It classifies the complexity based on the comparison between f(n) and n^log_b(a). The theorem has three cases to evaluate whether f(n) is polynomially smaller, equal, or larger than n^log_b(a). This theorem simplifies complexity analysis for algorithms like merge sort, binary search, and Strassen's matrix multiplication.

9 789369 727001

Printed at Repro India Ltd.